FOAM CRAFTS for kids

ISBN 978-1-4972-0401-0

© 2018 by New Design Originals Corporation, *www.d-originals.com*, an imprint of Fox Chapel Publishing, 800-457-9112, 903 Square Street, Mount Joy, PA 17552.

The Cataloging-in-Publication Data is on file with the Library of Congress.

Foam Crafts for Kids is a collection of new and previously published material. Portions of this book have been reproduced from *Foam Crafts on the Go* (978-1-57421-385-0), *Awesome Foam Craft* (978-1-57421-352-2), *Foam and Glitter* (978-1-57421-316-4), *Fun, Fun Foam 2* (978-1-57421-289-1), and *Strings 'n Things* (978-1-57421-293-8).

We are always looking for talented authors. To submit an idea, please send a brief inquiry to acquisitions@foxchapelpublishing.com.

Printed in Singapore
First printing

Shutterstock images: HannaMonika (2, 160 background); Africa Studio (4 top left); Maksim Lobanov (6–7); Dinga (8–9); jultud (10 top); Mark Rooks (10 bottom); pedphoto36pm (11); Lucie Lang (16 top right and top left, 64 top, 104 bottom); Enlightened Media (16 middle right, 68 bottom); ellinnur bakarudin (16 bottom right, 49 bottom); PhotobyE (16 middle left, 60 bottom right); Eshma (16 bottom left, 64 bottom); Natan86 (17 middle left); Marina Vlasova (17 background); Tomas Jasinskis (19 top left); Photo Melon (19 bottom right); DGLimages (20); ucchie79 (20–21 background); THONGCHAT MANMONTRI (52 bottom, 53 bottom left); Monkey Business Images (53 frame insert); Hogan Imaging (58 top frame insert); DGLimages (59 bottom frame insert); Phaendin (60 top and bottom frame inserts); Sergey Novikov (63 top frame insert); Rob Marmion (63 bottom frame insert); sumroeng chinnapan (75 sky background); severija (98 glitter background, 99 glitter background); elbud (102 bottom); nadtytok (106 bottom); Jiri Hera (109 top and bottom left); My Portfolio (118 bottom right); Olga Rom (132 bottom left and top right); Tony Campbell (133 bottom); Lev Kropotov (136 bottom); iofoto (139 bottom left); Freedon_Studio (144 bottom background); xpixel (151 bottom, 159); Vorobyeva (154 bottom left); Svitlana-ua (155 bottom); and Marcie Fowler - Shining Hope Images (157 bottom left).

FOAM CRAFTS for kids

Over 100 Colorful Craft Foam Projects to Make with Your Kids

Edited by Suzanne McNeill

with contributions from Lorine Mason, Margaret Riley, and Andrea Gibson

DESIGN ORIGINALS
an Imprint of Fox Chapel Publishing
www.d-originals.com

CONTENTS

6 Introduction

8 Getting Started

10 Craft Foam

10 Adhesives

15 Templates

16 Decorative Accents & Embellishments

19 Cutting

19 Rollers

20 Especially for Little Ones!

22 Useful Tips & Techniques

23 Interchangeable Embellishments

24 Projects

24 Fun in the Sun

26 Flowers

28 Stitch It!

30 Purple Desk Supplies

32 Pencil Holders

36 Pencil Toppers

42 Message & Reminder Boards

46 Butterfly Party!

52 Flower Power Party!

54 Foamy Flowers

57 Photo Keepers

64 Princess Room

68 Wild Animal Foam Shapes

72 Plant Pokes

75 Wind Socks

82 Handy Little Toys

88 Masquerade

98 Magical Accessories

105 Foamy Seasonal Fun

114 Land & Sea

121 On the Farm

128 Gift Boxes

132 Bags & Accessories

158 Index

160 About the Contributors

Introduction

Craft foam is perfect for children's projects. The range of colors, textures, and patterns available truly offers something for all ages, from solid basic colors to glittery sheets and precut shapes. Craft foam is easy to cut, and patterns can be traced directly onto its surface with little effort. It is readily available at craft, sewing, and discount stores, and the price is very budget friendly. Basically, crafting with foam is super easy, and avoids the mess that goes along with painting and other crafts! With just a handful of skills and techniques, children will soon be making their very own stylish and cool bags, purses, and accessories. Both boys and girls will love the range of projects in this book. Let the creativity begin!

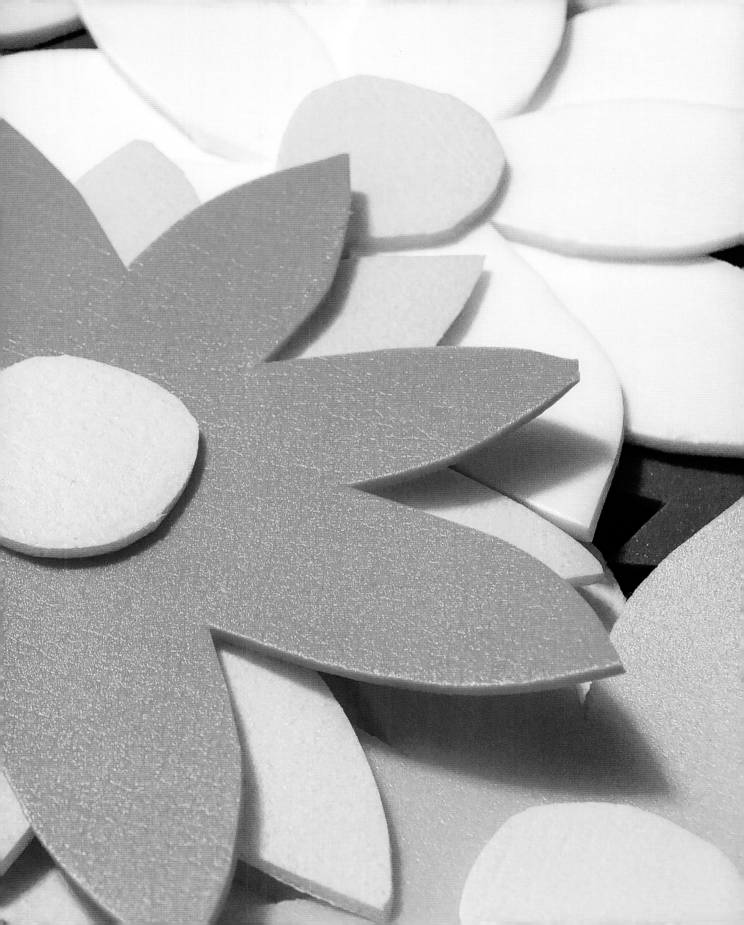

Getting Started

While you're still able to easily create fun and cool-looking foam crafts with just some scissors and glue, you'll definitely have more fun if you have other crafting materials and tools. This section will go over the essentials you will need to have on hand to complete the projects in this book. It also explains some techniques you will need to learn in order to have a fun and safe time while creating your foam projects. Once you learn the basics, the crafting can begin!

CRAFT FOAM

Craft foam is usually sold in thicknesses of 2 mm, 3 mm, and 5 mm. Thicker, sturdier sheets like the 5 mm are great for the important structural parts of projects, like bag sides. The thinner, more flexible 2-mm and 3-mm sheets are what most people think of when they think of craft foam, and are great for virtually everything else. The projects in this book were created using all three thicknesses; some foam material lists indicate 3-mm foam, but you can often interchange 3 mm and 2 mm as desired.

ADHESIVES

Adhesive choices are numerous and can be somewhat confusing. The reality is that there are certain stress points in these projects, and finding the correct adhesive ensures success. Stress points are the areas you want to pay close attention to and ensure good adhesion; they include corners and the areas where flaps, straps, and sides are attached to the sides of bags. Some of the best adhesive options include double-sided adhesive tape (extra strong), double-sided adhesive sheets (extra strong), sticky glue dots, sticky glue lines, and a low-temperature glue gun.

Using a low-temperature glue gun makes assembly of the projects quite fast, and the glue is suitable for use in all steps of the projects. However, even low-temperature glue guns can cause burns, and young children should not be left alone with these tools. While the glue coming out of the gun may not be considered hot, the nozzle on the glue gun can reach temperatures high enough to cause problems. The photographs in the book show the use of a low-temperature glue gun for constructing all projects. If you choose to use a glue gun, I would suggest that you work together with the child, setting the glue gun out of the child's reach, applying the glue to the craft foam, and then letting the child attach the craft foam sections one at a time.

There are many double-sided adhesive products on the market, but be sure to look for products that state they are suitable for adhesion to fabric, leather, and/or non-porous surfaces. Products used for paper crafting do not always have the amount of adhesion that is required for the projects in this book. This is especially important when dealing with high stress points such as flaps, sides, and pocket corners.

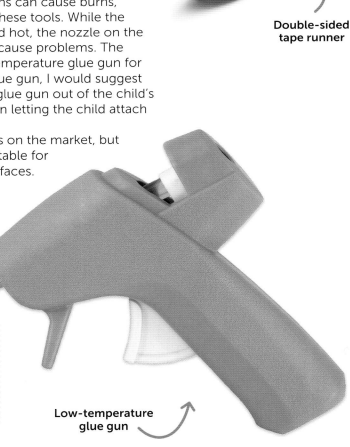

Double-sided tape runner

Low-temperature glue gun

WARNING: Read and follow all of the manufacturer's directions and guidelines before allowing children of any age access to a glue gun.

How to Use Double-Sided Adhesive Tape

1. Double-sided tape is great for attaching embellishments. Here, it is being used for a pocket. The orange strip is the backing (usually paper or plastic). First, apply the tape to your pocket (A).

2. Next, peel off the backing (B).

3. Finally, stick the pocket onto your piece (C). You're done!

4. Double-sided tape is also good for decorative accents. Apply the tape to the accent piece, then peel of the backing (D).

5. Attach the accent piece to your project (E).

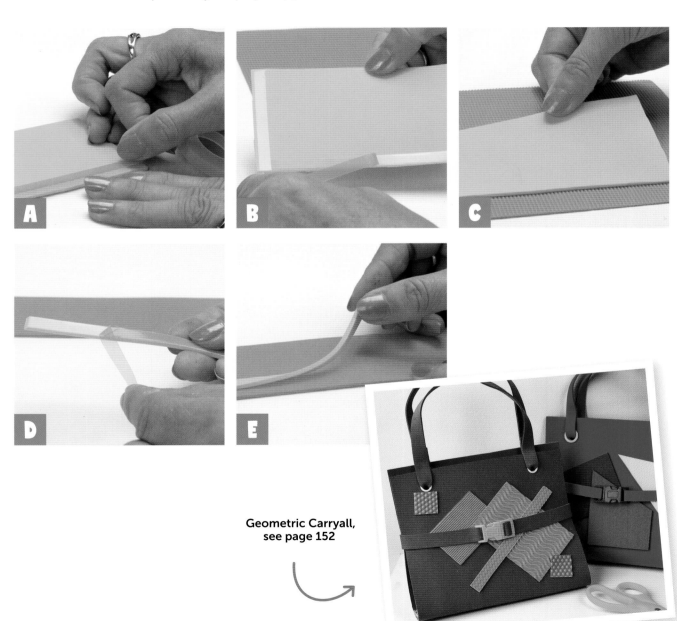

Geometric Carryall,
see page 152

How to Use Double-Sided Adhesive Sheets

1. If you want to attach adhesive to larger pieces of foam or want to die-cut adhesive-backed pieces, use double-sided adhesive sheets (A).

2. Simply press the sheet onto your foam piece and peel off one side of the backing as you go. When you are ready to attach the foam somewhere, remove the remaining backing as you go (B).

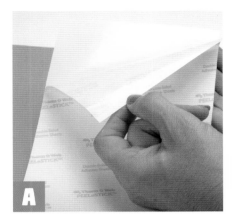

How to Use Sticky Glue Dots

1. Glue dots are great for adding smaller embellishments and pom-poms. First, peel off one layer of backing (A).

2. Press the embellishment against the glue dot (B).

3. Pull the embellishment, along with the glue dot, off the remaining layer of backing, and attach it to your piece (C).

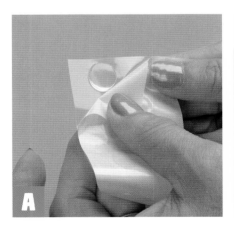
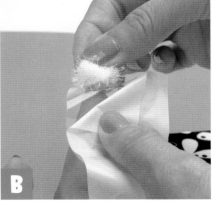

Sticky Glue Lines

1. Sticky glue lines have a stronger hold than double-sided adhesive tape, making them perfect for stress points like the sides of the bags. Peel one backing layer off the glue line first (A).

2. Stick the glue line onto the edges of your bag side (B).

3. Peel the other backing layer off the glue line (C).

4. Attach pieces to your bag side by pressing them onto the glue line (D).

5. This is a very simple, clean method (E).

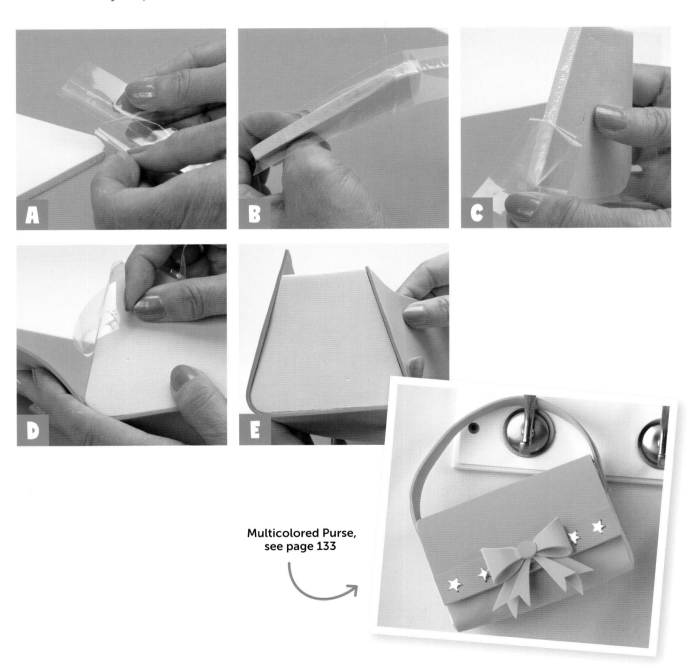

Multicolored Purse,
see page 133

TEMPLATES

The templates provided in this book can be easily photocopied directly onto card stock and cut out, or traced and then cut from cardboard to create a pattern tracer for children. If you're photocopying the templates, it's importnat to note that they do not need to be enlarged unless otherwise stated. Try gluing your template printouts onto cereal box cardboard and then cutting them out—that not only makes sturdy templates for children to trace around, but cereal boxes are fun and colorful, and you are reusing what would normally go in the trash!

How to Make Cereal Box Tracers

1. To make a sturdy pattern tracer from a cereal box, you need a photocopy of the template from the book, a tape roller, and your cereal box. When you cut out the paper template, you can leave extra space around it (A), because you'll be cutting that off in step 3.

2. Roll tape along the back of the paper template in multiple strips. It's okay to go over the template edges (B).

3. Stick the template on the back of your cardboard and carefully cut it along the lines (C).

4. Use a hole punch to mark straps or similar spots (D).

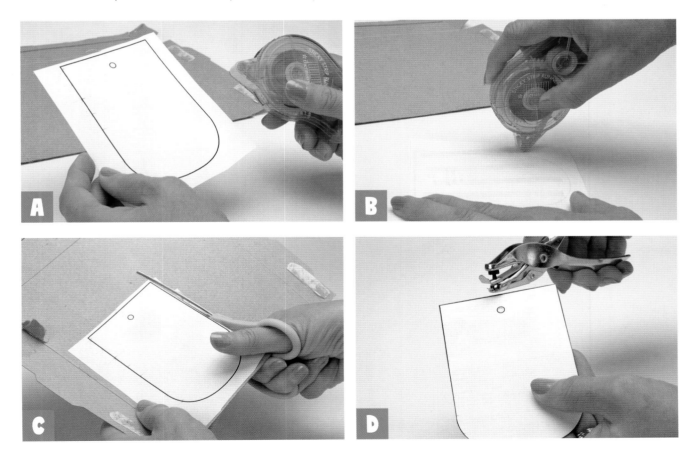

DECORATIVE ACCENTS & EMBELLISHMENTS

The options for embellishments are almost limitless! Check out the jewelry, paper crafting, sewing, and children's crafts sections in your local craft stores for ideas. Another option is to consider using repurposed, reclaimed, and recycled items. Here are just some of the items used for the projects in this book: permanent markers, plastic rings, beads, ribbons, plastic chain links, adhesive metallic dots, precut craft foam stickers, die-cut craft foam accents (using a cutting machine and select dies), buckles, brads, and swivel clips.

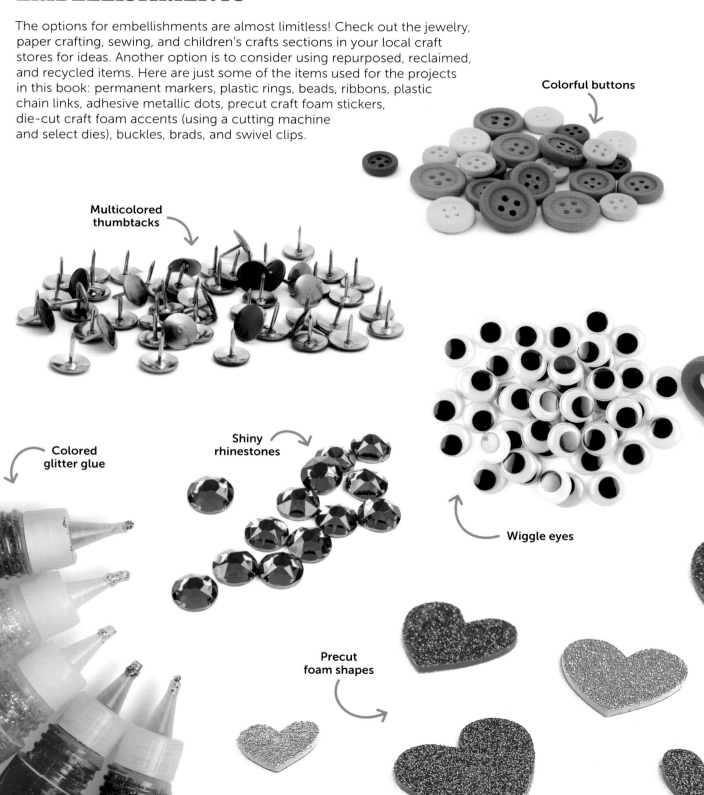

Colorful buttons

Multicolored thumbtacks

Colored glitter glue

Shiny rhinestones

Wiggle eyes

Precut foam shapes

How to Use a Die Cutter to Create Embellishments

You can add double-sided adhesive sheets to your foam pieces before cutting the shapes out for super easy stick-on embellishments. Below, learn how to use a simple crank-handle die cutter to do so.

    Note: Follow the manufacturer's instructions for your specific machine. Some machines use different items for layering, or are computerized and run automatically; familiarize yourself with your machine before beginning.

1. First, set up the plate, your foam, and the die, layered as shown (A).

2. Add the second plate on top, creating a sort of sandwich (B).

3. Feed the sandwich through the machine by turning the knob (C).

4. Here are your completed die cuts (D)!

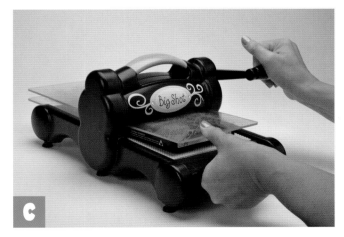

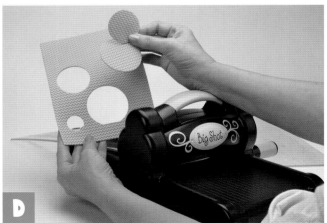

CUTTING

Cutting options are varied. A good pair of scissors is all that is absolutely necessary to cut out all of the pieces. When cutting the sturdy 5-mm craft foam and/or cutting curves, you might find it simpler to use a template and a craft knife. If you are considering making these items with a large group and need to prepare numerous pieces beforehand, consider pulling out your rotary cutter, mat, and ruler. Craft foam cuts beautifully using these tools, and you will be done in no time at all. Be careful not to allow children access to sharp craft knives.

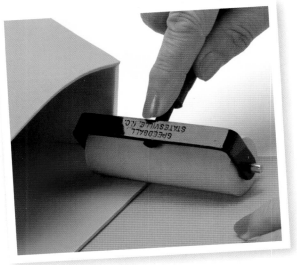

ROLLERS

This tip will ensure your bags look squeaky clean. You can use a roller to press two glued pieces together to achieve nice, smooth adhesion.

ESPECIALLY FOR LITTLE ONES!

Basic measuring, cutting, and gluing are all that is really needed to make every project in this book. Let the fun begin for the youngest children with embellishments. Older children can measure, cut, and glue their own purses and accessories from start to finish with a little supervision. Small children will want to create their very own version of many of the projects in this book. Embellishments are the key to success. Purchase a variety of adhesive-backed precut craft foam shapes, plastic jewels, ribbons, and beads. Set the stage by displaying the embellishments in dishes on the work surface alongside a finished sample of the project. Take a moment to explain how the children might use the embellishments, and then let them have at it! Depending on the project children are working on, give them one piece at a time to embellish. Try starting with a pocket to give them a chance to experiment. Depending on the type of adhesive you are using, most items are removable if taken off within minutes of their placement. Pass out additional sections of the projects to be embellished as the children work. Once all the pieces are decorated, assemble their projects quickly and easily using a glue gun while they continue with another game, activity, or snack. The projects in this book are perfect for parties for so many reasons: the projects, as well as the embellishments, can be themed; they are a fun crafting activity for groups; and the finished projects can be used as goodie bags by slipping some inexpensive toys or candies into the completed bags.

USEFUL TIPS & TECHNIQUES

Here are four additional techniques that will make it so much easier to make lovely, well-proportioned, and creative bags. Don't skip this section!

How to Line Up Hook-and-Loop Adhesive Dots

Eliminate the guesswork every time by following these instructions! You can use a roller to press two glued pieces together to achieve nice, smooth adhesion.

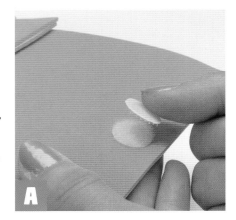

1. After attaching one half of the hook-and-loop adhesive dot to your bag flap, take the other half and place it on top of its partner (A).

2. Fold the flap down to close the bag and press the hook-and-loop closure into the bag body (B).

3. The other half of the dot will stick to the bag body aligned exactly where you want it (C).

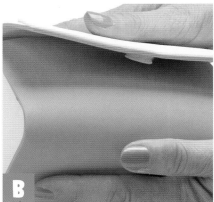

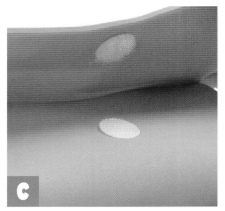

How to Use Brads

Here is the basic technique for applying brads to a project. When using brads, be careful of the sharp ends.

1. Poke the sharp end of the brad through your foam pieces (A).

2. If you are attaching one piece to another, as in the strap shown, insert the end of the brad through a premade hole (B).

3. Flatten the ends of the brad using an awl or similar tool (C).

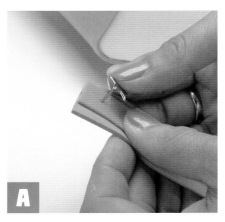

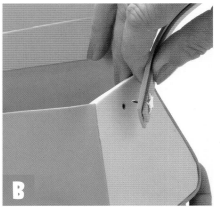

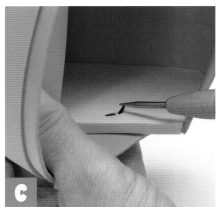

INTERCHANGEABLE EMBELLISHMENTS

One of the most fun things about making your own foam accessory is that you can customize its design any way you want. But what's even better than that? Being able to customize your item over and over again! With just a few simple steps, you'll be able to make embellishments that are removable, so you can change decorations in and out depending on your mood or style. That way, you won't ever have to worry about making the perfect piece, because you'll be able to change your piece any way you want. Try it!

1. Apply one half of a hook-and-loop adhesive dot to the place you want to create an interchangeable embellishment. Here, it is on the front of the bag flap (A).

2. Apply the other half of the hook-and-loop adhesive dot to the back side of your embellishment (B). You won't see the embellishment's hook-and-loop dot while it's attached, so it can be any color; it doesn't have to match the bag or even the other half of the dot!

3. Stick the embellishment onto your bag, and you're done (C).

4. Create as many removable embellishments as you like by layering precut foam shapes, cutting your own new shapes, and selecting pom-poms and jewelry (D). You can change your bag's look whenever you want.

LOVELY LADYBUG VISOR

Clever and cute, this ladybug will complete your look. It's perfect for keeping the summer sun off your face as you hang out by the pool with your friends.

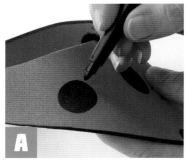

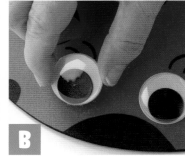

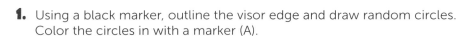

- 4"-wide red foam visor
- Black marker
- 1 black chenille stem
- 2 (30-mm) wiggle eyes
- ⅛" hole punch

1. Using a black marker, outline the visor edge and draw random circles. Color the circles in with a marker (A).

2. Glue the wiggle eyes in place (B). Draw eyelashes above the eyes.

3. Punch 2 holes for the antennae into the top rim of the visor, 2½" apart. Bend a chenille stem into a "U" and poke both ends through the holes from back to front. Swirl the antenna ends with your fingers (C).

WACKY CATERPILLAR VISOR

This bright visor is easy to make and adorable! The pom-pom antennae are super cool and really give the caterpillar a neat look.

- 4"-wide green foam visor
- Green foam pom-poms
- Foam adhesive-backed sheets in red, green, and light green
- Green marker
- 1 red and 3 lime green chenille stems
- 2 (20-mm) wiggle eyes
- ⅛" hole punch
- Glitter glue

1. Cut the adhesive-backed sheets into ½"-wide strips: 3 green, 2 light green, and 2 red. Trim to size and adhere to visor.

2. Cut the chenille stems to match each strip and adhere in place.

3. Add a wavy line of glitter glue to the foam strips. Let dry.

4. Glue the wiggle eyes onto the visor. Draw eye details below the eyes.

5. Punch two holes for the antennae 2" apart in the center of the visor's top rim. Bend the green chenille stem into a "U." Poke both ends through the holes from back to front.

6. Poke the green foam pom-pom onto the end of the chenille stick (B) and bend it into a loose swirl with your fingers.

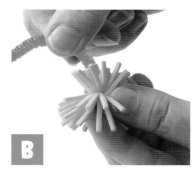

YELLOW DAFFODILS VISOR

Keep cool while you work in the flower garden with this daffodil visor. If daffodils aren't your favorite, change it up by using a different flower. You could even use a bunch of different ones in a multitude of colors to let your love of colors really shine!

- 4"-wide white foam visor
- 15 (1½"-diameter) yellow silk daffodils
- 15 white mini brads
- Pushpin

1. Using a pushpin, poke 15 holes evenly across the top rim of the visor (A).

2. Attach each silk flower with a brad (B). Make sure you poke the brad through the center of the flower.

3. Push brads open (C). Make sure to push the ends of the brads all the way down so they won't poke you when you put the visor on your head.

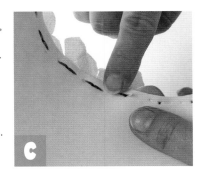

PERSONALIZED JOURNAL

Customize a journal for yourself, or make one as a gift for a friend. Create your journal using your favorite colors and shapes.

- 6" x 8" pink foam journal
- Craft foam:
  - 1 (4½" x 6½") white adhesive-backed sheet
  - 8 (⅜" to 1") blue and green precut flowers
  - ½" adhesive-backed letters
- 4 white mini brads
- Pink glitter glue
- 5 (⅝"-wide) pink floral ribbons, 4" long
- Pushpins

1. Adhere a white foam sheet to the book front. Trace the edge of the white foam with glitter glue. Let dry.

2. Poke a hole into two corners of the white foam with the pushpin, piercing the book. Layer the foam flowers by placing a small green flower on top of a larger blue one. Attach the flowers to the journal with the mini brads, piercing them through their centers.

3. Attach the other flowers (small blue on top, large green on bottom) through the pink foam on the opposite corners. Apply the adhesive-backed letters in alternating colors to spell out your name or a favorite quote. Tie ribbon pieces onto the journal's spine.

ALL-TIED-UP VISOR

Express your personal style with ribbons to match your favorite summer outfit. There are so many options to choose from, so you can really let your creativity soar!

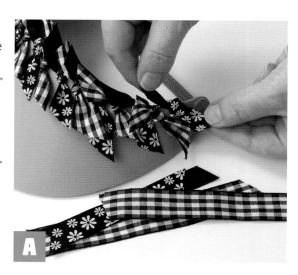

- 4"-wide pink foam visor
- 8 (⅝"-wide) black gingham ribbon, 4" long
- 9 (⅝"-wide) black floral ribbon, 4" long
- ¼" hole punch

1. Punch holes at ½" intervals around the top rim of visor.

2. Feed alternating ribbons through each hole and tie in a knot (A).

FLOWER FRENZY VISOR

Sweet and sparkling, this visor makes a bold fashion statement. The glitter glue is perfect for the summer since it really shines in the sun!

- 4"-wide black foam visor
- 1½" precut foam flowers: 3 pink, 3 purple, and 3 white
- Lavender glitter glue

A

1. Adhere the flowers to the front of the visor near the bottom rim.

2. Add lavender glitter glue to the flower center and then create radiating lines on each petal (A). Let dry.

3. Draw an outline around the flowers with lavender glitter glue. Let dry.

Stitch It!

CRAFTY VISORS

Whether you are cheering your favorite team or strolling the sandy beach, keep the sun out of your eyes and beat the heat with a cool visor.

- Prism craft thread
- Foam visor
- Adhesive foam shapes of your choice, or use the templates to create some of your own
- Size 18 needlepoint needle (which does not have a sharp point)
- Assorted buttons
- ⅛" hole punch

1. Plan out your design. Adhere your desired foam shapes to the visor and let dry.

2. Punch holes in the visor close to the rim and through the foam shapes.

3. Sew running stitches through the holes. Sew buttons to the visor. Experiment with your thread colors here. You can mix the colors for a single stitch or use multiple colors for stitching each shape; there are so many possibilities!

4. Punch holes around the buttons and then sew stitches around the buttons. Remember, you don't have to make each button look the same. Let your creativity reign free! Outline some with your stitches or make interesting patterns across others.

CUTE-AS-A-BUTTON COOZIE

When the summer heats up, keep your drinks cold with a personalized coozie. Go crazy with your design and put your stamp on it; that way you'll always know which one is yours!

- Prism craft thread
- Foam coozie
- Adhesive foam shapes of your choice, or use the templates to create some of your own
- Size 20 chenille needle (with a point sharp enough to pierce the foam coozie)
- Assorted buttons
- ⅛" hole punch

1. Punch holes in the foam shapes where you intend to create your stitches.

2. Plan out your design and adhere the shapes to the coozie.

3. Sew stitches through the holes, being careful not to poke yourself.

4. Glue the buttons in place. You can place them in empty areas around the coozie, or even on top of your embellishments.

5. Sew buttons to the coozie, again being careful not to poke yourself. If you like the look of the unsewn button, you could always skip over this step.

Flower templates

Bug templates

"NOTES" MESSAGE BOARD

It's easy to stay organized when you have a super cute message board to help you! Everyone will notice your important memos when written on this fun message board.

- 1 (7½" x 10½") dry erase foam flower board with marker
- Craft foam:
  - 1 green adhesive-backed sheet
  - 1 purple adhesive-backed sheet
  - 3 (¾") flowers
- Multicolored 6-mm pom-poms
- Foam paint: white, purple, and lime

1. Dip a small pom-pom in white paint and dab dots onto the foam flower board randomly. Let dry.

2. Add a purple paint dot to the center of each white dot. Let dry. Run a bead of adhesive around the marker board and add the multicolored pom-poms.

3. Trace the leaf pattern onto a green adhesive-backed sheet and then cut it out. Write the word "Notes" onto the leaf in white, adding details in lime foam paint (A). Let dry.

4. Adhere the leaf to the flower board back. Add some details with foam paint.

5. Cut a ½" strip of purple adhesive-backed foam. Peel and wrap it diagonally around the pen (B). Trim the ends to fit. Adhere 3 flowers to the covered pen.

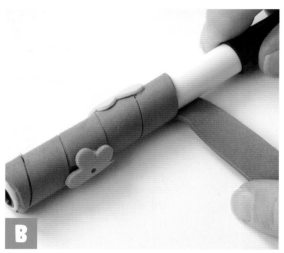

"Notes" leaf template

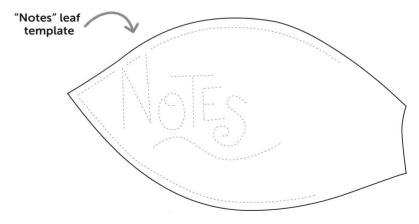

FAIRY-TALE PENCIL HOLDER

Using a variety of bead sizes and colors really sets this project apart. Make a pencil holder or drink coozie that is pretty enough for a princess.

- 1 (4" x 3½") purple foam coozie
- 6 adhesive-backed pink and purple castles
- 22-gauge non-tarnish silver wire
- Plastic bead assortment in purple and pink
- Pushpin
- Wire cutter
- Round-nose pliers

1. Poke holes evenly around the top of the coozie with a pushpin.

2. Cut 24" of wire. In one end, turn a loop and a small swirl.

3. Thread the wire through the first hole from the inside to the outside; add 4 to 5 beads; insert it through the next hole from the inside to the outside.

4. Repeat all around the coozie.

5. Finish off with a loop and a small swirl to secure the wire.

6. Add castles to the bottom of the coozie, trimming as needed to fit.

Castle template

GARDEN PENCIL HOLDER

If you're more of an outdoorsy person, how about storing garden supplies in one of these cheerful flower holders? This one is perfect for keeping your tools in one place.

- 1 (4½" x 3") round chip can
- Craft foam:
  - 1 (1½") dark pink octagon, for flower
  - 2 (¾") light pink octagons, for small flowers
  - 1 (¾") yellow circle, for large flower center
  - 2 (⅜") dark pink circles, for small flower centers
  - 2 (½" x ½") green teardrops, for leaves of large flower
  - 4 (⅜" x ⅞") green teardrops, for leaves of small flowers
  - 1 (¼" x 3") green piece, for stem
- Natural sponge
- Fine-tip black marker
- Light pink marker
- Acrylic paint: light blue and white

1. Paint the can light blue, then let it dry. Sponge white paint randomly over the can. You could even sponge the white paint to look like fluffy clouds in random spots on the can.

2. Draw light pink dots on the large dark pink octagon for the flower petals. You can add dots to the little octagon flowers with a different color, or leave them as a solid color.

3. Outline all foam shapes with a fine-tip black marker, keeping close to the edges as indicated on the patterns.

4. Glue the shapes to the box. The little flowers don't need stems; feel free to stick them just above the leaves.

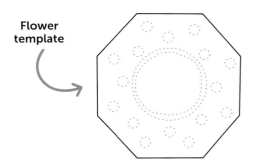

Flower template

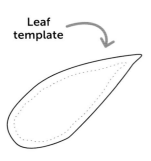

Leaf template

LOVABLE TURTLE PENCIL HOLDER

Fill an afternoon with productive fun, and make your pencils and colored pencils a new home. This pattern is for making three turtles, so if you'd prefer more turtles on your pencil holder, double or triple the foam materials!

- 1 (4½" x 3") round chip can
- Craft foam:
  - 3 (1¼"-tall) brown foam gingerbread men
  - 3 (¾") green foam octagons, for shells
- 6 (5-mm) wiggle eyes
- Natural sponge
- Fine-tip black marker
- Yellow marker
- Acrylic paint: light blue and dark blue

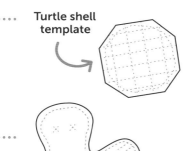

Turtle shell template

1. Paint the can light blue. Let dry.

2. Sponge dark blue paint randomly on painted can to mimic water. Let dry.

3. Draw yellow lines in a grid pattern on the shell of the turtle.

4. Outline all foam shapes with a fine-tip black marker. Draw toe lines and mark the eye placement as indicated on the pattern.

5. Glue the shells to the bodies and two eyes on the heads where you marked.

6. Glue the foam turtles to the box randomly or in a pattern . . . the choice is yours!

Turtle body template

SLITHERING SNAKE BOX

The perfect pencil holder for the aspiring herpetologist in your life! If you wanted to have more fun with this project, cut out and paint enough green foam ovals to wrap the snake around the box a couple of times in a longer zigzag pattern.

- 1 (2¼" x 2¼" x 3") chip box
- Craft foam:
  - 1 (⅜" x 1") green teardrop, for head
  - 6 (⅜" x 1") green ovals, for body
- Fine-tip black marker
- Acrylic paint: light blue, cherry red, and yellow
- Toothpick

1. Paint the can a very light blue (or any color that compliments green). Let dry.

2. Paint the cherry red and yellow dots on the snake's body with a toothpick. Four dots with each color works best. Keep your lines evenly spaced and consistent between all sections. Let dry.

3. Using the fine-tip black marker, draw the dashed lines on the oval body sections as indicated on the pattern.

4. Glue the shapes to the box in a fun zigzag pattern, as if the snake is slithering up the box's side.

Slithering Snake Box template

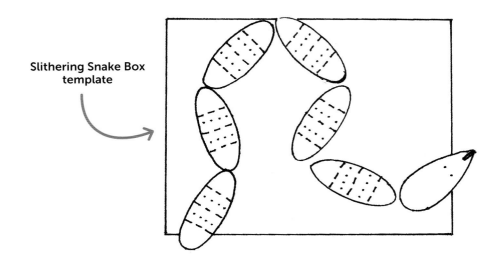

SUNSHINY FLOWER BOX

Don't forget, you can customize the flower and box colors to be anything you like. Choose your favorites, or match your room! You can even make multiple flowers in different colors or patterns so you just have to rotate the box when you're in the mood for a new color.

- **2¼" x 2¼" x 3" chip box**
- **Craft foam:**
  - **1 (1½") pink octagon, for flower**
  - **1 (⅜") purple circle, for large center**
  - **1 (¾") yellow circle, for smaller center**
  - **2 (½" x 1½") green teardrops, for leaves**
  - **1 (⅛" x 2") green rectangle, for stem**
- **Fine-tip black marker**
- **Fine-tip red marker**
- **Yellow marker**
- **Light blue acrylic paint**

1. Paint the chip box light blue. Let dry.

2. Draw the yellow dots onto the large pink octagon with a marker.

3. Outline the leaf and small flower center foam shapes with black marker. Outline the large pink octagon with the red marker.

4. Glue shapes to the box. If you wish to add more flowers to the box in different colors, create three more and glue them around the pencil holder.

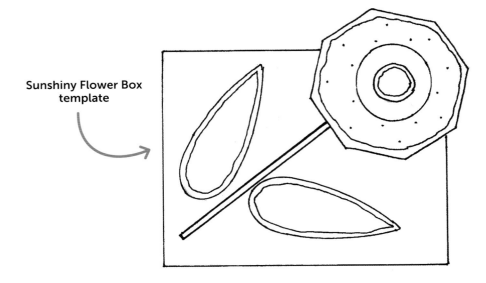

Sunshiny Flower Box template

BUSY BUMBLEBEE

Make your favorite pencil easy to find with this busy bumblebee pencil topper. This project goes great with the Garden Pencil Holder on page 32. The colorful foam shapes can also be used to embellish a box, frame, or notebook.

Busy Bumblebee template

- 10" 18-gauge wire
- Pencil
- Craft foam:
  - 2 large white hearts, for wings
  - 2 large yellow hearts, for body
  - 1 medium yellow heart, for head
- 2 (6-mm) wiggle eyes
- 3" 22-gauge silver wire
- Red chalk
- Fine-tip black marker

1. Trace the varying heart sizes onto your foam and cut them out.

2. Turn your medium yellow heart upside down and color in the cheeks with red chalk. Blend the color lightly with your finger to give your bee a cheerful, rosy look.

3. Following the template, draw and color in the thick black stripes with the black marker on the large yellow hearts. Start at the bottom of the heart and work your way up, keeping the lines even.

4. Outline the two large white hearts. Follow the template to draw in the curved lines so you end up with four wings.

5. Outline the face and draw on the smile with the black marker. Mark the spots where the wiggle eyes will go, then glue them onto the face.

6. Glue the wings onto the front body and the head on top of the wings.

7. Coil wire around pencil top, leaving 1" straight at the top of the wire.

8. Glue the back of body to the straight end of the wire, then glue the other large yellow heart to hide the wire.

9. Fold the silver wire in half and pull apart slightly to create a "V" shape. Wrap the ends of the wire around a paintbrush handle so you end up with a spiral. Glue the wire to the back of the bee's head to make antennae.

Body and wing template

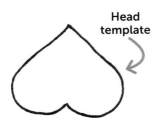

Head template

PRETTY BUTTERFLY

Your pencil will flutter like a butterfly with this colorful topper. If you'd prefer to have a sparkly butterfly, use more rhinestones or glitter glue to decorate it.

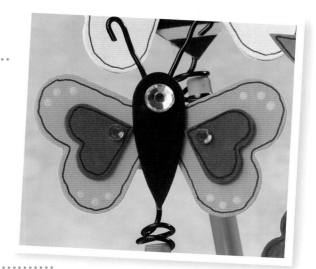

- 10" 18-gauge wire
- Craft foam:
  - 2 large pink hearts, for outer wings
  - 2 small purple hearts, for inner wings
  - 2 (⅝" x 1½") black teardrops, for body
- 1 (8-mm) clear rhinestone
- 2 (5-mm) pink rhinestones
- 3" 18-gauge black wire
- Pencil
- Fine-tip black marker
- Yellow marker

1. Trace your heart and teardrop designs onto the appropriate foam colors. Cut them out.

2. Glue the large rhinestone onto the thicker end of the black teardrop (the head) and the pink rhinestones near the tip of the purple hearts (inner wings). Create dots with the yellow marker on the curved areas of the large hearts.

3. Outline all pieces with the black marker.

4. Glue all pieces together, following the Pretty Butterfly template.

5. Fold a 3" wire in half and curl the ends. Glue it to the back of head. Let dry.

6. Coil a wire around a pencil top, leaving 1" straight at the top of the wire.

7. Glue the front body to the straight end of the wire, then glue on the second black teardrop to hide the wire between the two pieces.

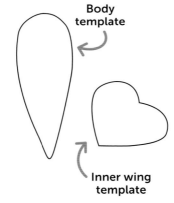

Body template

Inner wing template

Outer wing template

Pretty Butterfly template

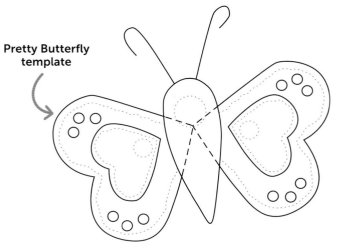

CUTE TURTLE

This adorable turtle looks just like a newly hatched baby sea turtle. Let him inspire you! Use your new pencil topper to write about his journey from the beach to the ocean and beyond.

- 10" 18-gauge wire
- Craft foam:
  - 1 (1½") brown gingerbread man, for body
  - 2 (¾") green octagons, for shell
- 2 (3-mm) wiggle eyes
- Pencil
- Fine-tip black marker
- Yellow marker

1. Trace the template images onto the foam and cut them out.

2. Draw the lines on the green octagon with the yellow marker. Outline all pieces with a black marker, keeping close to the edge. Draw in the feet lines, a dot for the nose, and mark where you will be placing the wiggle eyes.

3. Glue the eyes to the head and the shell to the body. Let dry.

4. Coil a wire around a pencil top, leaving 1" straight at the top of the wire.

5. Glue the front body to the straight end of the wire, then glue the second green octagon to the back to hide the wire.

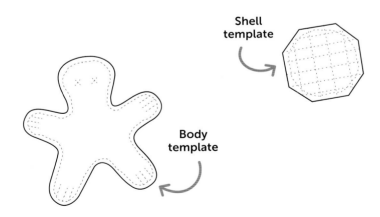

Shell template

Body template

POLKA-DOTTED FLOWER

This flower topper will have your pencil springing right up to meet your hand. Remember that you can customize your flower to your liking. Use your favorite colors and patterns so you'll smile every time you use it!

- **10" 18-gauge wire**
- **Craft foam:**
  - **2 (1½") pink polka-dotted octagons, for flower**
  - **1 (¾"-diameter) yellow circle, for flower center**
  - **2 (⅝" x 1½") teardrops, for leaves**
- **Pencil**
- **Fine-tip black marker**
- **Pink marker**

1. Trace the templates onto appropriate foam colors. Cut them out.

2. Outline all pieces with a black marker. Dab the dots on the flower with the pink marker.

3. Glue the yellow center to the front of the octagon and the leaves to the back of the octagon.

4. Coil a wire around a pencil top, leaving 1" straight at the top of the wire.

5. Glue the flower front to the straight end of the wire, then glue the second dark pink octagon to the back to hide the wire.

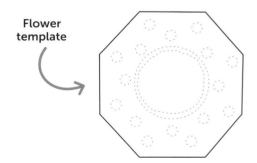

Flower template

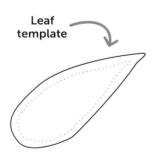

Leaf template

KISSY FISH

No need to fish your pencil out of the bottom of the box; this topper will make it easy to hook right away.

- **10" 18-gauge wire**
- **Craft foam:**
  - **2 (1⅜" x 2¾") green ovals, for body**
  - **Large yellow heart, for head**
  - **Medium orange heart, for tail fin**
  - **1 small orange heart, for fin**
  - **1 small red heart, for lips**
- **1 (10-mm) eye**
- **Pencil**
- **Fine-tip black marker**
- **Yellow marker**
- **Green marker**
- **Red chalk**

1. Trace the templates onto the foam. Cut them out.

2. Color cheeks with red chalk. Lightly blend with your finger to give your fish rosy cheeks.

3. Outline all pieces with a black marker. Draw the lip, fin, tail lines, eyes, and eyebrows, following the template. Draw dots on the head and body with the green and yellow markers.

4. Glue the lips and the wiggle eye to the yellow head. Then, glue the head and the small orange fin to the front of the front body. Glue the large orange tail fin to the back of the front body.

5. Coil a wire around a pencil top, leaving 1" straight at the top of the wire.

6. Glue the back of the front body to the straight end of the wire, then glue the other green oval to back of body to hide wire.

Fish head template

Tail fin template

Lips and side fin template

Fish body template

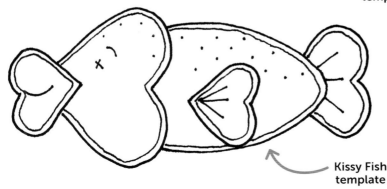

Kissy Fish template

MINI ME BLACKBOARD

Do you leave notes on the kitchen counter or your bedroom door? Make a blackboard to hold them. Dress up a kid with buttons, belt buckles, or rhinestones to make a mini version of yourself!

- 1 (5" x 7") blackboard
- Mini dowel, for chalk
- Flesh-colored and gray foam
- ⅞" foam letter stickers
- 4" jute hair curls
- ⅛"-wide pink ribbon, 10" long (optional)
- Fine-tip black marker
- Acrylic paint: yellow, magenta, light pink, dark blue, and white
- Red chalk

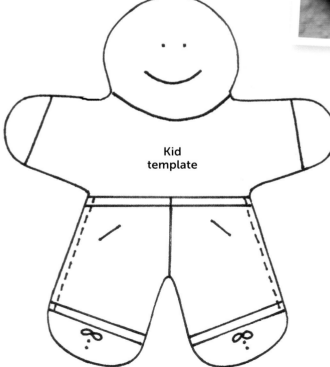

Kid
template

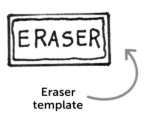

Eraser
template

1. Cut two pieces of the mini dowel ⅞" long for the chalk.

2. Paint the blackboard frame yellow. Let dry.

3. Cut out the foam pieces. Color the cheeks with red chalk, gently blending with your finger to give your mini-self rosy cheeks.

4. Outline the blackboard frame with the black marker using dashes and dots.

5. Paint the shirt with magenta acrylic paint; let dry. Do the same to paint the light pink polka dots on the shirt, the dark blue on the jeans, and the white on the shoes.

6. Draw lines for the sleeves, collar, pants seams, pants line, pockets, and shoelaces using the black marker. Draw a smile from cheek to cheek and two large dots for eyes.

7. Outline and write "ERASER" on the rectangle.

8. For short hair, glue 1½" of hair on the head. For longer hair, glue curly hair around the edges. Optional: For two ribbon bows, glue one on the hair and one on the neck.

9. Glue the figure, the dowel chalk, eraser, and the name letters to the blackboard, following the image.

SPORTY SCHEDULE HOLDER

This sports activity magnet is just what you need to keep track of all your games and practices! Hang it on your refrigerator or in your room so you'll see it all the time and never be late again.

- 1 (12" x 18" sheet) royal blue craft foam sheet (cut 5" x 18")
- Craft foam (9" x 12" sheets):
  - 1 brown, for pennant flag pole
  - 1 white (cut 1 soccer ball, 1 baseball, and 2 football stripes)
  - 1 cream (cut 1 baseball bat)
  - 1 light brown (cut 1 football)
  - 1 orange (cut 1 basketball)

- 1 green (cut 1 sports flag)
- Glitter foam:
  - 2 gold glitter stars (1½" precut or use star B template)
  - 1 blue glitter star (1½" precut or use star B template)
  - 8 gold glitter stars (1" precut or use star A template)
  - 2 blue glitter stars (1" precut or use star A template)

- ⅝" foam adhesive-backed letters
- 3 (1¾") wood clip-style clothespins
- 1 (4½" x 13½") magnetic adhesive sheet
- Acrylic paint: lamp black and cherry red

1. Paint lamp black lines on the basketball, football, and bat. Paint cherry red lines on the baseball for the stitching. Paint the pentagonal and half-pentagonal shapes on the soccer ball lamp black.

2. Glue brown craft foam for a pennant's stick onto the green pennant flag. Add your name to the pennant with the adhesive-backed foam letters.

3. Glue a magnet sheet to the back side of the blue craft foam, then glue white stripes to each end of the football.

4. Glue one clothespin to the center of the blue craft foam along the lower edge and the remaining two clothespins approximately 2" from each side edge.

5. Glue on the pennant and sports items.

6. Glue the glitter stars onto the clothespins. Add the remaining glitter stars around the pennant and sports items.

Sporty Schedule Holder Templates

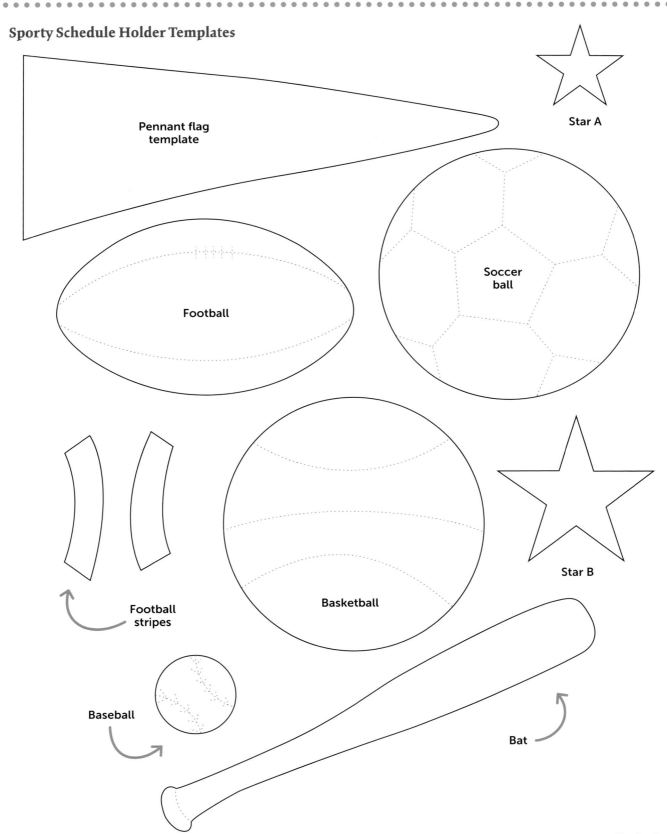

Pennant flag
template

Star A

Soccer
ball

Football

Football
stripes

Basketball

Star B

Baseball

Bat

BUTTERFLY GARDEN CENTERPIECE

Make a beautiful centerpiece for your butterfly party with these gorgeous foam creations. You could even put them outside your house to greet your guests. Stick them right in the dirt of your garden or flowerbed, or put sand in a flowerpot to show off your colorful butterfly garden. These directions will create six daisies and six butterflies, so make more for a larger centerpiece.

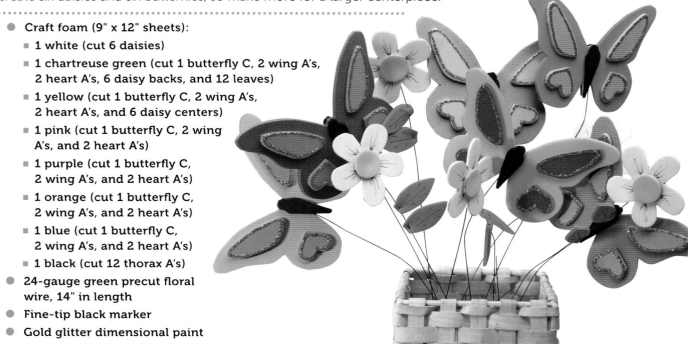

- Craft foam (9" x 12" sheets):
  - 1 white (cut 6 daisies)
  - 1 chartreuse green (cut 1 butterfly C, 2 wing A's, 2 heart A's, 6 daisy backs, and 12 leaves)
  - 1 yellow (cut 1 butterfly C, 2 wing A's, 2 heart A's, and 6 daisy centers)
  - 1 pink (cut 1 butterfly C, 2 wing A's, and 2 heart A's)
  - 1 purple (cut 1 butterfly C, 2 wing A's, and 2 heart A's)
  - 1 orange (cut 1 butterfly C, 2 wing A's, and 2 heart A's)
  - 1 blue (cut 1 butterfly C, 2 wing A's, and 2 heart A's)
  - 1 black (cut 12 thorax A's)
- 24-gauge green precut floral wire, 14" in length
- Fine-tip black marker
- Gold glitter dimensional paint

Note: See pages 50–51 for the templates.

1. Glue the yellow daisy center to the daisy. Glue the floral wire to center back of the daisy as if it were a stem. Glue the daisy back over the end of the wire to hide it.

2. Poke the wire into the flat end of the leaf twice and push up. You can change up the leaf positions from flower to flower.

3. Use a marker to add lines to the leaves and daisy petals.

4. Lay a floral wire on the thorax of the butterfly and glue a butterfly shape over it, sandwiching the wire in between.

5. Glue a thorax on other side so the wire and the butterfly shape are between the two thorax pieces.

6. Glue the hearts and wing details on the butterfly shapes, let them dry, and then outline them with gold glitter.

7. Repeat all of these until you have six daisies and six butterflies. When complete, stick the wires into your desired centerpiece. (Floral foam in a decorative basket will work great!)

SPRINGTIME BUTTERFLY NAPKIN RINGS

The little details count! Create these wonderful butterfly napkin rings to give your party a sophisticated look that will leave your guests feeling impressed. The directions below will create one napkin ring.

- Craft foam (9" x 12" sheets):
  - 1 white, for napkin ring base
  - 1 white (cut 1 butterfly C)
  - 1 green (cut 2 wing A's and 2 heart A's)
  - 1 black (cut 1 thorax A)
- Gold glitter dimensional paint

Note: See pages 50–51 for the templates.

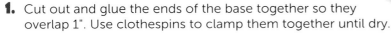

1. Cut out and glue the ends of the base together so they overlap 1". Use clothespins to clamp them together until dry.

2. Trace and cut out all templates: 1 white butterfly, 2 green wing details, 2 green hearts, and 1 black thorax.

3. Glue the thorax, hearts, and wings onto the butterfly. Outline the edges of the wings and hearts with glitter paint.

4. Glue the ring to the back of the butterfly.

STYLISH BUTTERFLY PENCIL FAVOR

This perky butterfly on a pencil is a great gift to make for your friends or give as a favor at your next party.

- Craft foam (9" x 12" sheets):
  - 1 pink (cut 1 butterfly C)
  - 1 purple (cut 2 wing A's and 2 heart A's)
- Gold glitter dimensional paint
- Pencil
- ⅛" ribbon, 14" long: orange satin, yellow satin, pink satin, yellow picot satin, and purple grosgrain

Note: See pages 50–51 for the templates.

1. Trace and cut out 1 pink butterfly, 2 wing details, and 2 hearts.

2. Glue the wings and hearts on butterfly.

3. Use a knife to cut two lines for the pencil insertion.

4. Outline the wings and hearts with glitter paint.

5. Tie the ribbon on the pencil.

FAIRY BUTTERFLY CROWN

Wearing this crown makes it easy to pretend you're a fairy! Make one for each of your guests so you can all let your imaginations roam free together.

- Craft foam (9" x 12" sheets):
  - 1 pink (cut 4 butterfly A's)
  - 1 orange (cut 1 star)
  - 1 yellow (cut 1 star)
  - 1 purple (cut 2 stars)
- ⅛" ribbon, 1 yard long: orange satin, yellow satin, pink satin, and purple grosgrain
- ⅝"-wide yellow/orange butterfly print satin ribbon, 1 yard long
- Gold glitter dimensional paint
- Wired cording or tinsel

Note: See page 51 for the templates.

1. Outline each butterfly in gold glitter dimensional paint.

2. Measure the wired cording or tinsel around your head and twist the ends together to form a circle. Alternate gluing the butterflies and stars onto a circle, using clothespins until the glue dries.

3. Loop and secure the ribbons onto the circle.

SWEET BUTTERFLY STRAW

Make these for your partygoers' drinks so you'll all have straws that match your theme. Perch the charming creatures on your straws so you see it every time you take a drink.

- Craft foam (9" x 12" sheets):
  - 1 purple (cut 1 butterfly B)
  - 1 yellow (cut 2 wing B's)
  - 1 chartreuse green (cut 2 wing C's)
- Gold glitter dimensional paint
- Drinking straw

Note: See page 51 for the templates.

1. Glue wing designs onto butterfly. Use a knife to cut two slits to insert the straw into the butterfly.

2. Outline each wing with glitter paint.

GLITTERY HEART BUTTERFLY MASK

Use the bold colors and patterns shown or study some butterflies on your own and adapt the project to match them. Make one for each of your guests; you'll not only have fun with your own butterfly masquerade, but they'll be able to take them home afterward!

- 1 (12" x 18" sheet) lavender (cut 1 butterfly mask on fold, so it creates an entire butterfly)
- Craft foam (9" x 12" sheets):
  - 1 green glitter (cut 2 heart B's)
  - 1 gold glitter (cut 2 heart D's)
  - 1 blue glitter (cut 2 heart D's)
  - 1 purple glitter (cut 2 heart D's)
  - 1 fuchsia glitter (cut 2 heart C's)
  - 1 black glitter (cut 1 thorax B)
- Gold glitter dimensional paint
- 3" of gold metallic chenille stem
- 2 wooden tongue depressors

Note: See page 50 for the templates.

1. Cut out the heart openings on the butterfly mask as marked on the template. Glue on the thorax and hearts as shown in the picture.

2. Cut one tongue depressor to 4¼" and glue to the back of the mask on the thorax. Glue the other tongue depressor below the first, extending it at least 3" below the body.

3. Use gold glitter to add dots and swirls as on the picture or in a pattern of your desire.

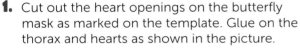

Butterfly Party Templates

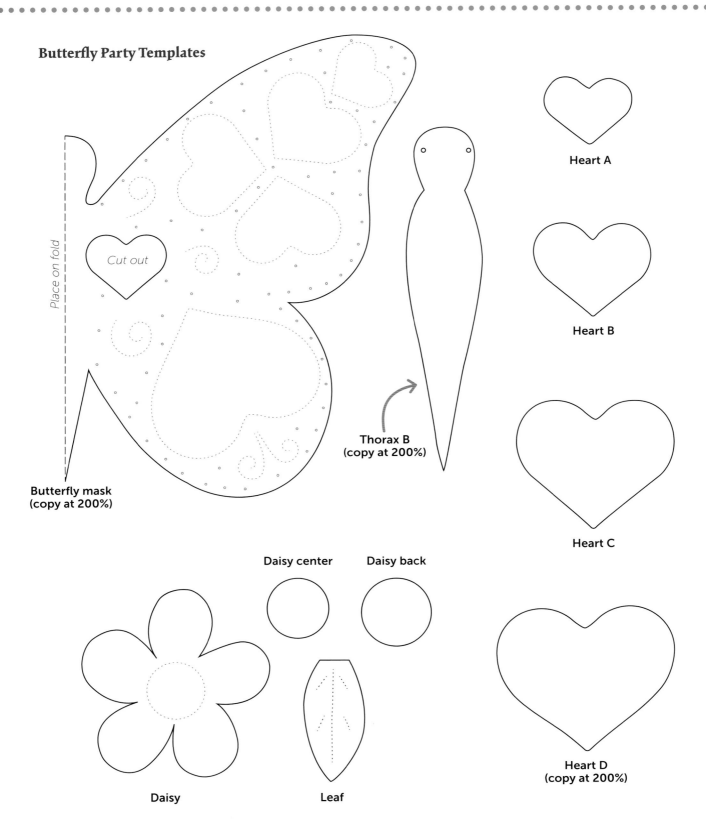

Place on fold

Cut out

**Butterfly mask
(copy at 200%)**

**Thorax B
(copy at 200%)**

Heart A

Heart B

Heart C

Daisy center

Daisy back

Daisy

Leaf

**Heart D
(copy at 200%)**

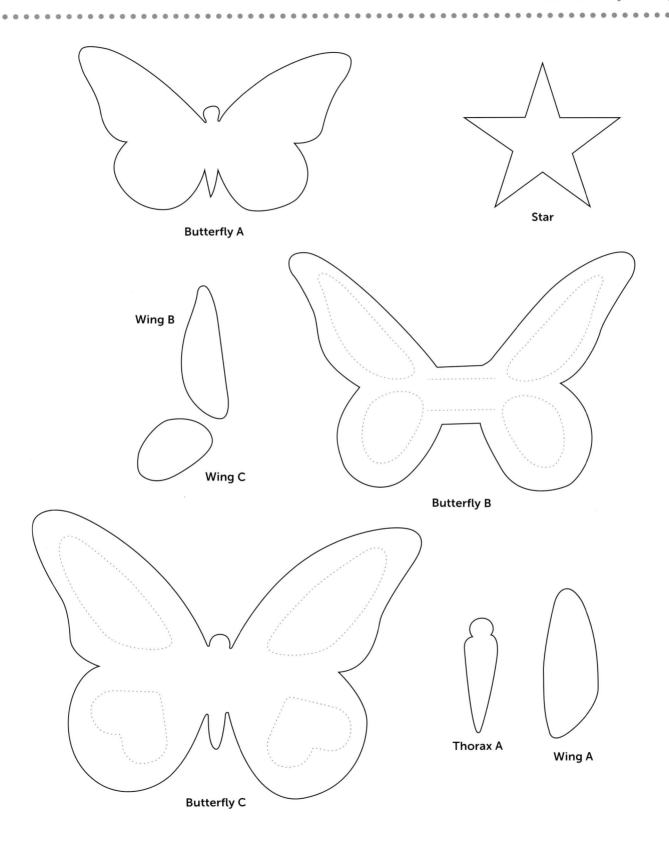

Butterfly A

Star

Wing B

Wing C

Butterfly B

Butterfly C

Thorax A

Wing A

Flower Power Party!

Get the party started with matching invitations, seat markers, and frame favors. These projects are perfect for sleepovers and birthday parties.

- **Craft foam:**
  - 1 (8" x 11") pink adhesive-backed sheet
  - 1 (3" x 3") white adhesive-backed sheet
  - 2 (1") teal adhesive-backed circles
  - 4" x 6" pink or teal magnetic foam frame
  - ¾" pink foam letters
  - 4 small and 4 large adhesive-backed flowers: pink and white
- **Foam flower block stamp**
- **10 teal 9-mm rhinestones**
- **½"-wide ribbon, 8" long: 3 pink, 3 white, and 3 striped**
- **Precut foam letters (2" to 3"), for each guest's first initial**
- **Rub-on letters**
- **1 (8" x 11") white card stock**
- **Black marker**
- **Fuchsia craft paint**
- **Crop-A-Dile punch**
- **Sponge brush**

A

1. Apply fuchsia paint to the foam flower stamp with a sponge brush. Stamp randomly over the pink foam sheet and the seat marker foam letters (A). Let dry.

For the invitations:

2. Cut out 2 tag shapes in 4½" x 8½". Cut the remaining flowers from leftover foam. Print or write invitation details on card stock. Peel the backing from the pink tags and apply them to the back of the printed card stock, carefully lining up the words with the tag. Trim the card stock to fit the tag. Repeat for each tag. Adhere the cutout stamped foam flowers inside as desired.

3. Place the tags together, with the teal circles at point. Punch holes through the circles and tags. Tie with ribbons. Sandwich each ribbon end between two flowers.

4. Adhere the white square on the cover, draw a black dotted line with a foam marker, and adhere the foam letters. Accent the letters with a black foam marker (B). Glue rhinestones to the flower centers as desired.

B

For the seat markers:

5. Apply rub-on letters to name each person attending the party on the precut foam letters. Glue teal rhinestones to the flower centers as desired.

For the frame:

6. Apply fuchsia paint to the foam flower stamp with a sponge brush. Stamp randomly over the frame. Let dry. Glue teal rhinestones in the middle of whole flowers as desired. Insert a favorite party photo to remember the fun time you all had together.

PURPLE PANSY

This would be a great project for Easter, Mother's Day, or any other spring holiday. Make more than one and place them around your house to show that spring has sprung!

- ● **Lavender foam flower shape**
- ● **Green adhesive-backed foam sheet**
- ● **Chenille stems in lime green and purple**
- ● **8 small pom-poms**
- ● **Pushpin**
- ● **Wire cutters**

1. Trace the flower leaves and stem onto the back of the green adhesive-backed sheet. Cut them out.

2. Stick the shapes onto a flower form, covering the lavender leaves and stem.

3. Cut the purple chenille stems into five 4½" pieces. Bend a right angle in the last ¼" of each end (A). Form a flower petal.

4. Poke two holes toward the middle of each flower petal with a pushpin.

5. Thread the ends of the purple stem into holes and press down on the back of the flower (B). Repeat for each petal.

6. Cut two green chenille stems 6" long. Apply them to the leaves as with the petals.

7. Glue yellow pom-poms to the center of the flower (C).

SPECIAL HOMEMADE CARD

There's no better way to tell someone you care than by making him or her a card. You can always make a similar one with different shapes and colors to suit the receiver.

- ● **18 (⅜" to 1") foam flowers**
- ● **1 (5" x 8½") white card stock**
- ● **1 (4" x 5") striped paper**
- ● **9 white minibrads**
- ● **Rub-on words (the sample uses "There is no one like you")**
- ● **Chalk ink**
- ● **Pushpin**

1. Fold the card stock in half. Cover the front with striped paper. Cut an uneven wave along the front of the card. Ink all card edges.

2. Poke holes ½" apart along the bottom of the card front. Layer foam flowers, varying size and color, and attach them to the card with mini brads.

3. Add the rub-on words to create your desired message.

THERE IS NO ONE LIKE YOU

BRIGHT FLOWER BRACELETS

Soft, pretty, and fun to wear, everyone is going to want one of these flower bracelets! The best part is that they're so easy to make.

- Foam flowers, sized between ⅜" and 1"
- 1-mm stretchy cord
- 8-mm and 6-mm bicone beads (the sample uses pink and orange)

1. Measure the wrist, adding 2" for tying off.

2. Make a knot at one end of the stretchy cord so your flowers and beads stay on the cord.

3. String one bead, four flowers, one bead, and four flowers. Repeat until the cord is full.

4. Tie the ends securely and trim the ends.

FLOWERED INITIAL SIGN

Initials are a hot decorating item. This project is a fun activity for any party or to decorate your room!

- Foam letter
- Foam flowers, sized between ⅜" and 1"
- ¾" ball-head straight pins
- Neon sequins

1. Pair a foam flower with a sequin. Pin it into the foam letter with a ball-head straight pin (A).

2. Repeat this process until you've covered the foam letter completely with flowers.

A

CAT & MOUSE MAGNETIC FRAME

This playful frame is perfect for your school portraits and other small photos!

- Purple and pink foam sheets
- Pom-poms: 1 (1½") black, 1 (1") black, 1 (1") white, 3 (10-mm) white, 2 (5-mm) pink, and 13 (5-mm) light blue
- Chenille stems: 1 (6-mm) black and 1 (3-mm) pink
- White and pink felt
- 4 (5-mm) wiggle eyes
- Magnetic strip

1. Cut the foam pieces using the frame template. Use zigzag scissors to give the edges of the purple square a fun design.

2. Put glue on three edges of the purple square. Center it on top of the pink square, leaving one side unglued so you can slip in your photos.

3. Glue light blue pom-poms around the opening.

4. Assemble the cat and mouse and glue them to the frame.

5. Glue the magnet on the back, stick in your picture, and hang on the fridge.

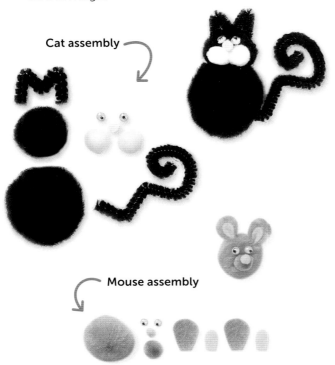

Cat assembly

Mouse assembly

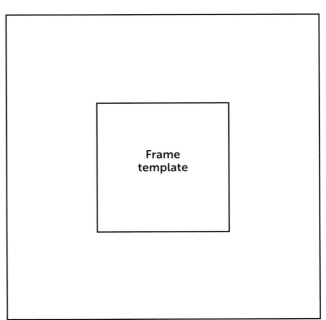

Frame template

MERRY MOUSE MAGNETIC FRAME

You can never have enough photo frames, and you can never have too many magnets!

- White and yellow foam sheets
- Pom-poms: 1 (1") gray, 1 (10-mm) gray, 1 (10-mm) yellow, and 1 (5-mm) pink
- Chenille stems: (6-mm) hot pink and (3-mm) pink
- Gray and pink felt
- 2 (5-mm) wiggle eyes
- Magnetic strip
- White paper
- ¼" hole punch
- Fine-tip black marker

Note: See page 57 for the template.

1. Cut the foam pieces using the frame template and punch holes in the yellow piece so it looks like Swiss cheese.

2. Using the triangle template below, trace and cut out the triangle on a piece of white paper. Write "Say cheese!" on the paper.

3. Assemble the mouse and flag following the picture. Glue both to the frame.

4. Glue the magnet on the back.

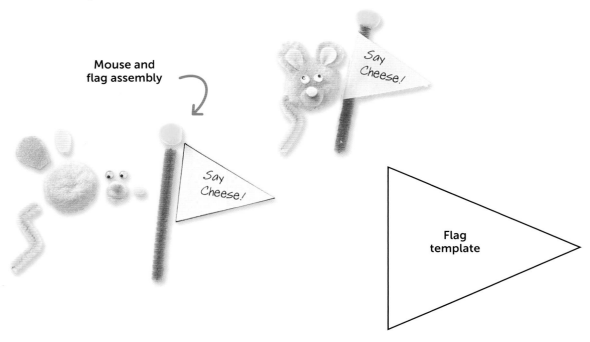

Mouse and flag assembly

Flag template

"SOME BUNNY LOVES YOU" MAGNETIC FRAME

Instead of a photo, you could also write a special message inside the frame. Or frame a ticket stub or other scrap of paper you want to keep!

- Pink and yellow foam sheets
- Pom-poms: 1 (1") white, 2 (½") white, 2 (10-mm) white, 1 (¾") orange, 1 (½") orange, 1 (10-mm) orange, and 1 (5-mm) pink
- Chenille stems (6-mm): hot pink, pink, green, and white (bump)
- 2 (5-mm) wiggle eyes
- Magnetic strip
- White paper
- ¼" hole punch
- Fine-tip black marker

Note: See page 57 for the template.

1. Cut the foam pieces using the frame template.

2. Punch holes into a yellow piece of foam and collect the circles they produce. Glue the yellow circles onto the frame.

3. Bend a piece of pink chenille so it lines the opening of the frame, and glue it there.

4. Assemble the bunny and carrot. Glue both to the frame.

5. Write "Some bunny loves you" on a piece of paper. Glue it behind the opening.

6. Glue a magnet on the back.

Bunny assembly

Carrot assembly

LADYBUG LOVE MAGNETIC FRAME

Make a magnetic frame for mom, dad, grandparents, teachers, and everyone else on your list! They make a perfect gift with your latest school photo inside.

- Purple foam
- Pom-poms: 2 (1") red, 2 (½") black, 4 (5-mm) red, and 14 (3-mm) black
- 3-mm chenille stems: black and green
- 4 (4-mm) wiggle eyes
- Magnetic strip

Note: See page 57 for the template.

1. Cut out the foam pieces using the frame template.

2. Assemble two ladybugs.

3. Glue the bugs and grass to the frame. Center and glue your picture into the opening.

4. Glue a magnet on the back.

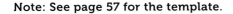

Ladybug assembly

PRINCESS SCRAPBOOK PAGE

Foam is safe and acid-free for your scrapbook projects. Incorporate this beautiful dimensional technique into your pages just for fun. Optional: change the word to your name!

- **Craft foam:**
  - 1 (2½" x 7") purple adhesive-backed sheet
  - 1 (2" x 2") green adhesive-backed sheet
  - Adhesive-backed flowers: 3 purple and 2 white
  - ½" purple sparkle letters
- 1 (12" x 12") double-sided green card stock
- 5 purple 8-mm rhinestones
- Opal glitter glue

1. Cut the card stock to 8" x 8" and 4" x 6".

2. Cut the pieces from the purple foam strip to form a mosaic border, keeping pieces in order as you cut. Apply them to the 8" card stock as a border, leaving room for "Princess" at the top.

3. Cut leaves from the green adhesive-backed foam. Peel and stick the leaves and flowers to embellish the page.

4. Glue rhinestones to the flower centers.

5. Add additional details to the flowers with opal glitter glue. Let dry.

6. Apply the letter stickers above the photo to form the word "Princess."

RAFTIN' THE RIVER FRAME

Relive the fun! Display your fabulous vacation photos in a photo keeper that is as fun as the trip.

- Yellow and green 4" x 6" foam photo keeper
- 3 green foam bugs
- 2 yellow foam bugs
- Pony beads: 11 green, 11 yellow, and 11 gold
- 6 (¼"-wide) green ribbons, 4" long
- Green jelly roll pen
- Crop-A-Dile punch

1. Punch 11 holes across the bottom of the keeper cover ½" apart.

2. Tie a knot in the end of one ribbon, add three beads, then insert the ribbon in the first hole. Knot (A).

3. Ribbon 2: Knot the end, string three beads, thread down through second hole and up through third hole, add three beads, and knot.

4. Repeat the above step to complete the beaded edge (B).

5. Give your photo keeper a name. Write and doodle around the frame with a green pen (C).

6. Stick a green bug on the cover.

7. Adhere more bugs to the individual pages to form tabs (D).

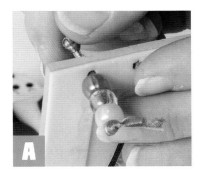

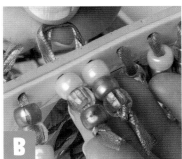

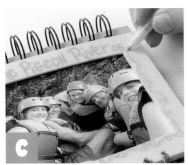

LIME FUN FRAME

Quick, easy, and fun, rub-ons provide endless possibilities for giving a frame its own unique style. Rhinestones add both a glittering shine and a 3D look.

- Lime foam frame
- Rub-on flowers
- Adhesive-backed rhinestones in blue and green
- ⅜"-wide green ribbon, 28" long
- Hole punch

1. Rub on flowers randomly (A). Add rhinestones to a few select flower centers.

2. Punch a hole in the top corners of the frame. Thread the ribbon through the holes and tie a bow for hanging.

CHEERY CATERPILLAR FRAME

Foam critters sparkle on this cute frame. Spell out your name with foam letters or make this frame for someone else, spell out their name, put in a picture of you two, and give as a gift!

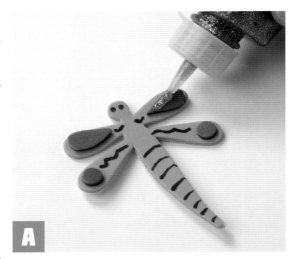

- 1 (4" x 6") blue magnetic frame
- White adhesive-backed foam letters
- Green foam caterpillar
- Green-blue foam dragonfly
- Opal and blue glitter glues
- Black, blue, and white foam markers
- 4" silver 22-gauge non-tarnish wire
- Wire cutters
- Round-nose pliers

1. Outline the circles on the caterpillar body with a marker, alternating white and blue. Draw a smile and antennae. Use glitter glue to accent the body. Glue the caterpillar to the frame.

2. Outline the white letters with a blue marker and stick them to the frame.

3. Cut the wire into two 2" pieces. Make antennae by turning a loop with round-nose pliers into each wire end, then swirl. Poke the other end directly into the dragonfly's head. Add details onto the dragonfly (A) and stick it to the frame.

PRINCESS TIARA

Crown yourself as the princess of the fairy realm with a personalized flowered tiara. Make sure to use a variety of colors to make this tiara really stand out!

- Pink foam tiara
- 10 (⅜" to 1") multicolored precut foam flowers
- ½" foam adhesive-backed letters
- 5 white mini brads
- Pushpin

1. Poke holes across the top of the tiara on the points.

2. Layer the foam flowers, varying size and color, and attach them to the tiara with mini brads.

3. Apply the letters to spell out your name.

ENCHANTED STAR WAND

Complete a royal ensemble with a sparkling star wand. This project will go great with the Princess Tiara. You'll be ruling the realm in no time at all!

- 1 (4½") pink precut foam star
- ¼"-diameter dowel rod, 12" long
- ¼"-wide ribbon, 24" long: pink and white
- Pink acrylic paint
- Silver glitter glue

1. Paint the dowel pink. Paint the star with glitter glue, adding swirly designs and dots. Let dry.

2. Poke a dowel into the base of the star to make a hole. Apply glue to the tip of the dowel and insert it into the star. Let dry.

3. Wrap ribbons around dowel at the base of the star.

"KNOCK, PLEASE" DOOR HANGER

"Knock, please," because there's a genius at work. Make a colorful door sign for your room to let people know this is your room!

- Pink flower foam door hanger
- Pink silk hydrangea petals pulled from stem
- Yellow and pink brads
- Foam stamp letters
- Raspberry craft paint
- Black marker
- Sponge brush
- Pushpin

1. Apply raspberry paint to the foam letters with a sponge brush (A). Stamp onto the door hanger below the flower. Let dry.

2. Outline letters and write "please" with a black marker.

3. Poke holes around the inside of the flower.

4. Layer two flower heads together and attach with a brad (B).

A

B

SPARKLY LINK CHAIN

This chain is so easy to make and so fun to use! You can wear it around your neck or hang it on furniture to brighten a room. You could also turn this into seasonal decorations by using certain colors, such as orange and black for Halloween or green and red for Christmas.

- ¾" x 4½" strips of glitter craft foam from various colors
- Clothespins

1. Glue the ends of one strip together to form a loop. Use clothespins until dry.

2. Insert the next strip through the loop and glue them so the loops chain together.

3. Repeat until the chain is as long as you want it.

MAGICAL FAIRY DOOR

Create a fairy door to attach to the base of a tree or in the back of your closet. Pretending fairies are all around us is soothing to the soul!

- Craft foam (9" x 12" sheets):
  - 1 light brown, for fairy door
  - 1 yellow, for fairy window
- Ruler
- Pen or fine-tip marker
- ½" gray button

1. Use a ruler to draw the board lines onto the door and the dividing lines onto the yellow window.

2. Glue the window and the button to the door.

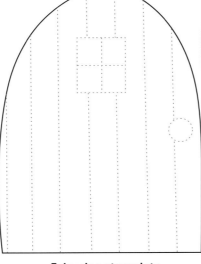

Window template

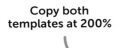

Copy both templates at 200%

Fairy door template

Wild Animal Foam Shapes

SEQUINED FISH

Sequins transform into sparkling fish scales on this clever project. You can turn it into an ornament for your window by poking a small hole in the top and running a string through it. Hang and watch it sparkle in the sun!

- Precut teal fish foam shape
- Lime sequins

1. Draw scalloped rows on the body and lines on the tail fin with glue. Let dry according to package directions.

2. Apply lime sequins to the dried glue. Repeat on the opposite side if you'll be hanging this project in the window to let it sparkle on both sides.

SWIRLY BLUE DOLPHIN

A fun addition to any room! Go wild with the glitter glue on this project, connecting swirl after swirl, to create a really cool-looking dolphin.

- Precut blue dolphin foam shape
- Small wiggle eye
- Opal glitter glue

1. Using opal glitter glue, draw random doodles and squiggles onto the dolphin. Let dry.

2. Glue on the wiggle eye.

GLITTERY SEAHORSE

Add some themed sparkle to your room or party! Take your time with creating the glitter glue designs to make sure you get it just right.

- Precut teal seahorse foam shape
- Small wiggle eye
- Teal, copper, and purple glitter glues
- Toothpick (optional)

1. Apply the glitter glue to the seahorse's body in a scaly pattern with the different glitter glues. Apply lines to the back fin and the "hair" around the head. Add dots at the crown of the head. To avoid smearing, allow the glitter glue to dry between adding the glue to each area of the seahorse's body.

2. Adhere the eye to the seahorse's face. Add tiny dots around the eye with varying colors of the glitter glue. (It might help to use a toothpick for this part.)

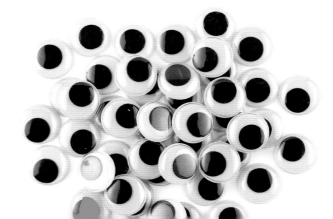

BRIGHT BUTTERFLY

Add a bit of summer to your room with this bright butterfly.
Make more than one to experiment with your color combinations.

- **Precut pink foam butterfly shape**
- **Black adhesive-backed foam sheet**
- **Chenille stems: 2 pink, 2 blue, 2 orange, and 1 lime green**
- **2 small wiggle eyes**
- **Green foam marker**
- **Wire cutters**
- **Round-nose pliers**
- **Pushpin**

1. Poke holes evenly around the outside of the butterfly wings.

2. Lace around wings with chenille stems, threading from the bottom to the top (A).

3. Fold ends down on back of butterfly.

4. Cut 5" of green chenille stem, fold in half, swirl ends, and glue to butterfly as antennae.

5. Cut a black foam body and stick in place.

6. Form butterfly wings with orange chenille stem following the picture (B).

7. To secure shaped orange stems to butterfly, cut 2 orange stems 1" long, then bend into a "U."

8. Make two holes in each side of the butterfly body.

9. Capture the shaped stem under the "U" and push the ends of the "U" through to the back of the butterfly and bend down.

10. Color in a portion of the black body with green foam marker.

11. Glue on wiggle eyes.

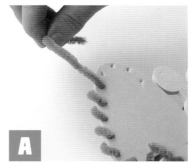

A

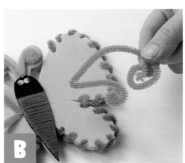

B

STITCHED ANIMAL CARDS

Lacing cards are easy to make. Glitter foam gives extra pizzazz and choosing contrasting colored thread will really make your animals stand out!

- Craft thread
- Craft foam or glitter foam shapes
- ¼" and ⅛" hole punches
- Size 18 needlepoint needle

1. Punch holes in a foam shape around its border.

2. Stitch through the holes. You can choose to which stitch to sew: a cross-stitch, running stitch, or whipstitch. Follow along with the stitch tutorial images for your desired technique.

Running stitch

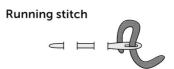

Cross-stitch

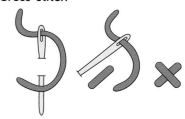

Whipstitch

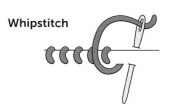

Stitched Animal Cards Templates

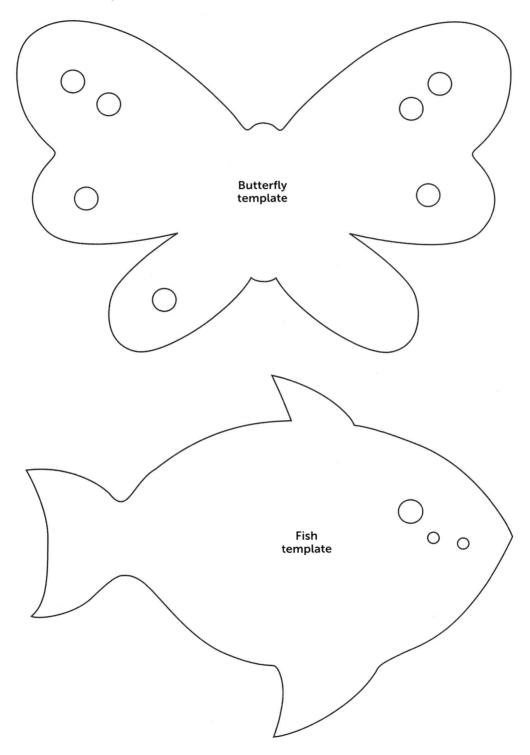

Butterfly
template

Fish
template

SCARLET CARDINAL

These cardinals will brighten your yard with their dazzling red color. The bright red is sure to be a beautiful contrast to all of the green plants that will surround it!

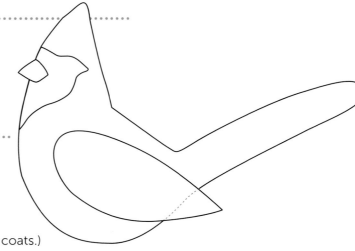

- Craft foam:
  - 1 (3" x 6") red sheet
  - 1 (3" x 6") black sheet
- 12" twig
- 2 black 4-mm half round beads, for eyes
- Black and gold foam paint

1. Cut out two copies of each cardinal piece using the template to the right.

2. Glue the twig between both body pieces.

3. Glue one wing on each side.

4. Paint the entire beak gold. (You may need multiple coats.)

5. On both sides, paint the face area black. Let dry.

6. Glue one eye bead on each side. Let dry.

WILD ROBIN

Robins bring spring! But you can enjoy them all season long with this garden decoration. Use a longer stick to place this bird among the taller plants in your garden.

- Craft foam:
  - 1 (4" x 6") brown sheet
  - 1 (4" x 6") orange sheet
- 12" twig
- 2 black 4-mm half round beads, for eyes
- White and gold foam paint

1. Cut out two copies of each robin piece using the template to the right.

2. Glue a twig between both body pieces.

3. Glue one breast, one wing, and one eye bead on each side.

4. Paint the entire beak gold. (You may need multiple coats.)

5. On both sides, paint the neck areas above the breast white. Let dry.

IRIDESCENT DRAGONFLY

Glistening wings add sparkle to your flowers. You can use nearly any color for the dragonfly's body, so let your creativity soar!

- **Craft foam:**
  - 1 (2" x 6") white sheet
  - 1 (2" x 6") turquoise sheet
- **12" twig**
- **Opal and turquoise glitter glue**

1. Cut out two copies of each dragonfly piece using the templates to the right.

2. Glue the twig between the wings and body.

3. Add sparkle to the wings and body with glitter glue. Follow the pattern in the image, or make up your own!

DAINTY LADYBUG

Ladybugs are a welcome guest in any garden! Create this plant poke and put it in your garden to encourage visits from this little insect.

- **Craft foam:**
  - 1 (2½" x 2½") red sheet
  - 1 (2½" x 2½") black sheet
- **12" twig**
- **Black foam marker**
- **Black foam paint**

1. Cut out two copies of each ladybug piece using the template to the right.

2. Draw the centerline on the red body piece.

3. Glue the twig between the top and bottom layers.

4. Add some spots with black paint.

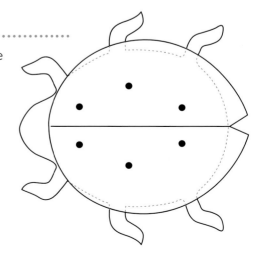

Wind Socks

HAPPY-GO-LUCKY WIND SOCKS

Invite the breeze over to play with these charming wind socks. Make a Croaky Frog, a Zany Zebra, a Merry Reindeer, and a Smashing Pumpkin for whimsical, windy fun!

For the Croaky Frog:

- Craft foam:
  - 2 (12" x 18") Kelly green sheets
  - Yellow, black, and red sheets
  - 14 (¹³⁄₁₆") and 7 (1¼") lime green precut circles
  - 2 (1⅝") red hearts
  - 2 small lime green precut hands (cut off thumbs)
- 48" of black 1-mm macramé cord
- 1"-wide Kelly green ribbon, 6 yards long
- Gold, burgundy, and forest green chalk
- 2½" and 3½" circle templates (eyes)
- ⁵⁄₁₆" (nose) and 1¼" (eyes) circle punches

For the Zany Zebra:

- Craft foam:
  - 1 (12" x 18") zebra print sheet
  - Black and pink sheets
  - 2 (1⅝") magenta precut hearts
- 48" of black 1-mm macramé cord
- Ribbon:
  - ⅝"-wide white ribbon, 4 yards long
  - ⅝"-wide black ribbon, 1½ yards long
  - ⅜"- wide black ribbon, 1½ yards long
  - 1"-wide black ribbon, 1½ yards long
- Black, purple, and fuchsia chalk
- 1" circle punch (black eyes and nostrils)

Projects | **75**

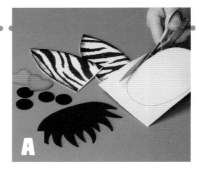

For the Smashing Pumpkin:

- Craft foam:
  - 1 (12" x 18") orange sheet
  - Black, yellow, green, and brown sheets
  - 2 (¹³⁄₁₆") purple precut circles
- 1-mm black macramé cord, 48" long
- 1"-wide orange ribbon, 6 yards long
- Green permanent marker
- Gold, rust, Kelly green, and forest green chalk
- ¼" circle punch (for eyes)

TIP: Cut the black foam for the eyes, nose, and mouth just a little bit larger than the yellow foam pieces.

For the Merry Reindeer:

- Craft foam:
  - 1 (12" x 18") brown sheet
  - Black, tan, white, and brown sheets
  - 1 (1⅝") red precut heart
- 2 (1¼") white precut flowers
- 48" of black 1mm macramé cord
- 1½"-wide brown ribbon, 4 yards long
- Red, brown, and burgundy chalk
- 1" circle punch (black eyes)

Note: See pages 78–80 for the templates.

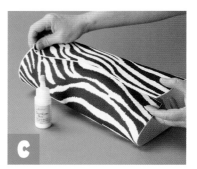

1. Gather the precut shapes. Cut the facial features and shapes needed for the wind sock you're making (A). Shade the edges of the shapes and a 12" x 18" sheet of foam with chalk.

2. Place the sheet right side up. Mark the center points of the long edges. Using marks as guides, glue facial features, hair, and ears to the center of the foam sheet (B).

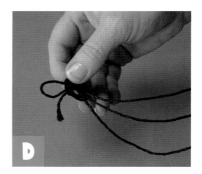

3. Roll the sheet into a tube, overlap the ends, and glue to secure (C). Use clothespins to hold the seam in place until the glue dries.

4. Cut one 16" and one 32" piece of cord. Fold the long cord in half. Place the 16" cord with the 32" cord and tie an overhand knot in the folded end (D). Cut the end of the 16" cord close to the knot; dot with glue.

5. On the wind sock's top edge, place a mark 2¾" from each side of the center. Glue the cord end to each mark and back to the seam. Glue foam circles over the cord ends (E). Cut the ribbon into 18" pieces. Glue to the bottom edge, leaving ¾" between. Let dry, hang, and enjoy!

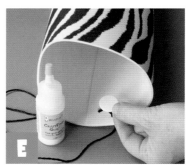

TROPICAL WIND SOCK

Create a tropical wind sock to enjoy yourself or give as a gift. It's a great reminder of how much fun it is to be at the beach!

- ● Craft foam (12" x 18" sheets):
  - ■ 1 blue (cut 1 piece 7" x 18" and 4 pieces ½" x 1½")
  - ■ 1 chartreuse green (cut 1 fish D; cut 3 danglers 1¼" x 12"; cut seaweed)
  - ■ 1 lavender (cut 3 danglers 1¼" x 12")
  - ■ 1 yellow (cut 1 fish C; cut 3 danglers 1¼" x 12")
- ● Craft foam (9" x 12" sheets):
  - ■ 1 dark green (cut 1 fish D fins; cut seaweed)
  - ■ 1 medium green (cut seaweed)
  - ■ 1 tan (cut 1 sand)
  - ■ 1 turquoise (cut 1 fish C fins)
  - ■ 1 light pink (cut 1 fish B)
  - ■ 1 dark pink (cut 1 fish B fins)
  - ■ 1 white (cut 1 each fish A, B, C, and D eyes)
  - ■ 1 orange (cut 1 fish A)
  - ■ 1 light orange (cut 1 fish A fins)
- ● Dimensional paint: black, green, glue glitter, crystal glitter, and green glitter
- ● Acrylic paint: lamp black
- ● Variety of small seashells
- ● ¼"-wide chartreuse green satin ribbon, 3 yards long

Note: See page 81 for the templates.

1. Paint all details on all fish parts lamp black. Add details to all leaves, using green between leaves and green glitter for leaf veins.

2. Glue on the sand and leaves. Use brown dimensional paint to add lines to the sand.

3. Glue seashells on the sand. Glue the fins, eyes, and tails to the fish. Glue on the fish. Add bubbles of blue and crystal glitter dots.

4. Glue the danglers evenly around bottom of the wind sock. Glue the side seam with a slight overlap. Use clothespins at top and bottom until dry. (Hint: Lay seam side down and put something with some weight to it over the seam to help hold it together until dry.)

5. Use a large hole punch to make four ¼" holes evenly along top, approximately ⅜" from top edge. Glue small blue strips over the holes. Repunch the holes.

6. Cut the ribbon into four equal pieces. Loop a ribbon through the hole. Bring loose ends up and tie all together, leaving 4" of ribbon hanging loose. Tie two loose ribbons together to create a loop for hanging.

Happy-Go-Lucky Wind Socks Templates

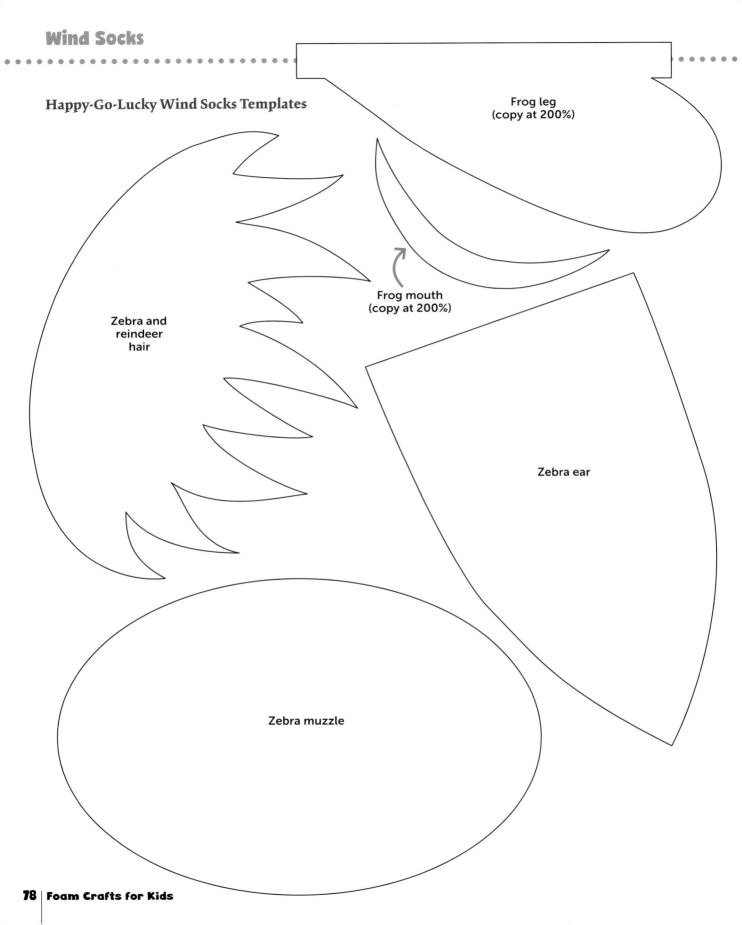

Frog leg
(copy at 200%)

Zebra and
reindeer
hair

Frog mouth
(copy at 200%)

Zebra ear

Zebra muzzle

Happy-Go-Lucky Wind Socks Templates

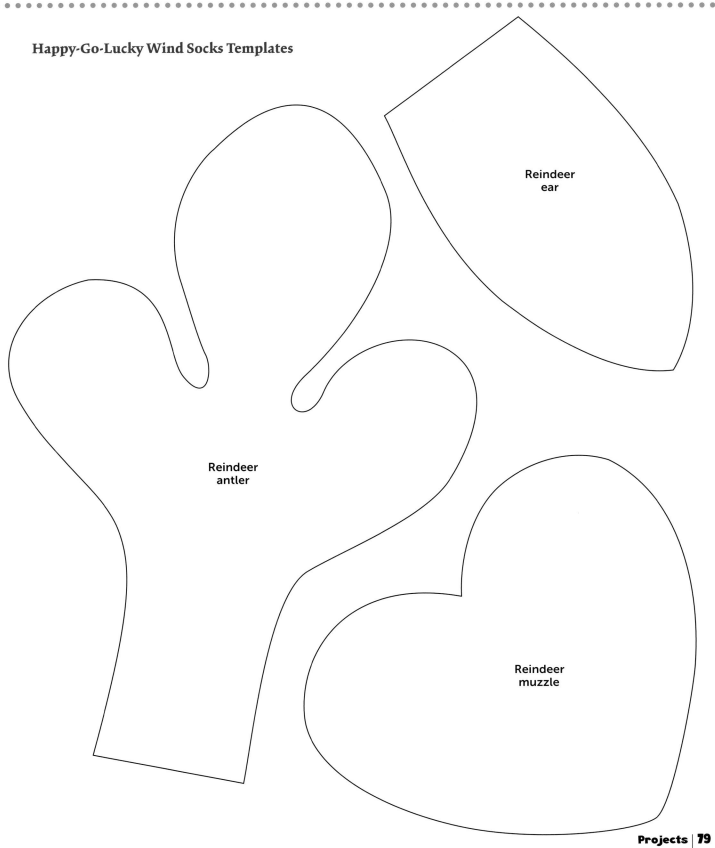

Reindeer
ear

Reindeer
antler

Reindeer
muzzle

Happy-Go-Lucky Wind Socks Templates

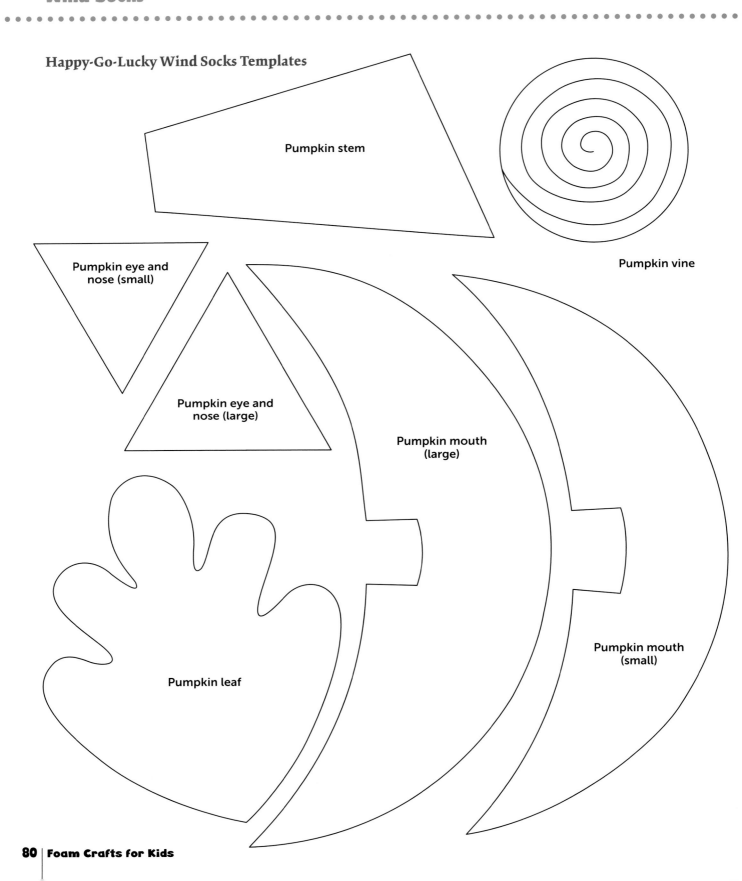

Pumpkin stem

Pumpkin vine

Pumpkin eye and nose (small)

Pumpkin eye and nose (large)

Pumpkin mouth (large)

Pumpkin mouth (small)

Pumpkin leaf

Tropical Wind Sock Templates

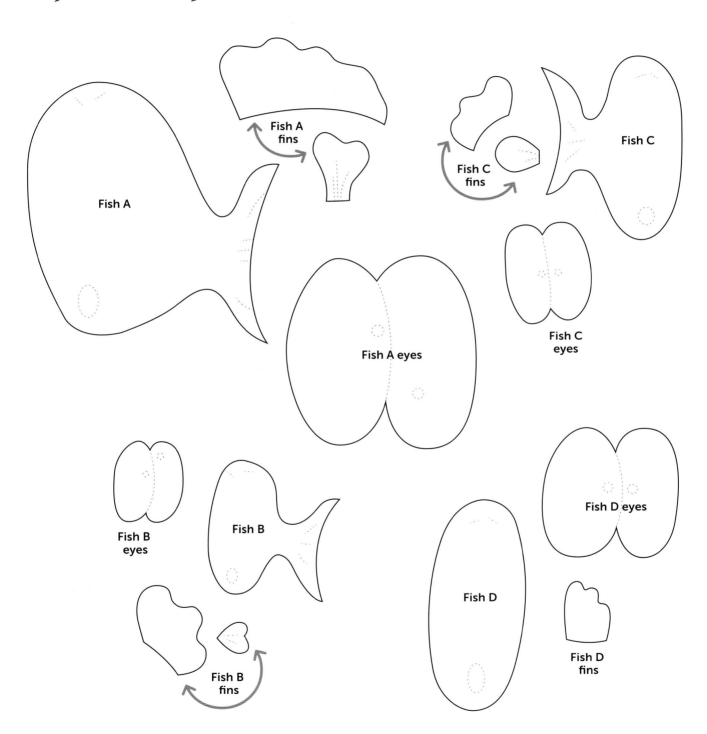

Fish A fins

Fish A

Fish A eyes

Fish C fins

Fish C

Fish C eyes

Fish B eyes

Fish B

Fish B fins

Fish D eyes

Fish D

Fish D fins

FINGER PUPPET FAMILY

Create a story with finger puppets. This great activity created by Kathy Wegner is perfect for a scout meeting or just hanging out with your friends on a rainy day.

- Craft foam:
  - 4 (4" x 5") sheets (yellow, blue, green, and red)
  - 2 (4" x 4") sheets (tan and peach)
  - 2 (1" x 2") sheets (orange and black)
  - 1 (2" x 3") dark brown sheet
  - 1 (2½" x 2½") light brown sheet
- Foam markers (black, pink, and red)
- 3 (⅜") white buttons
- Assorted seed beads
- White foam paint
- Glitter glue

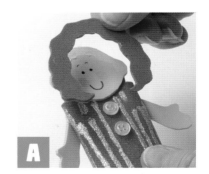

A

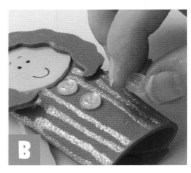

B

1. Using the templates, trace the designs onto the foam and cut out.

2. Follow Diagrams A and B on the next page to glue tabs to form bodies. Glue the tops of the heads together.

3. Adhere the faces, hair, and arms to the body (A).

4. Draw facial features with markers.

5. Decorate the bodies with glitter, buttons, and beads (B).

Finger Puppet Family Templates

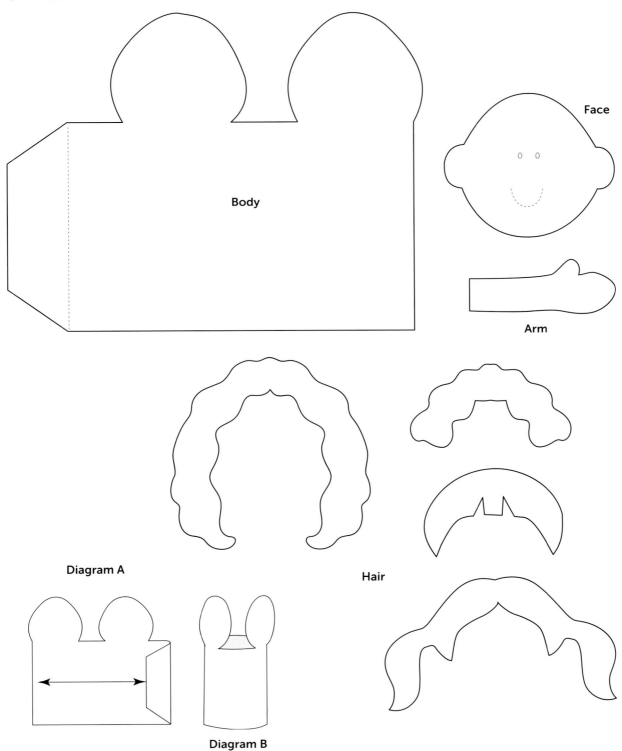

Body

Face

Arm

Diagram A

Hair

Diagram B

MORE FINGER PUPPET FUN!

Now that you have a taste for the puppet theater, branch out with more outlandish characters!

For the Spooky Jack-o'-Lantern:

- Black, orange, green, and brown foam
- ⅜" green precut foam heart
- 3" of green 3-mm chenille
- Black, green, and red markers
- ⁵⁄₁₆" and 1" circle punches

TIP: Cut the green heart in half to make leaves.

For the Striped Cat:

- White, yellow, red, and black foam
- 3" of yellow 6-mm chenille
- Brown watercolor marker
- Black thread
- ⅛", ⁵⁄₁₆", and 1" circle punches

For the Pink Rabbit:

- Pink, white, black, magenta, and turquoise foam
- 3" of pink 3-mm chenille
- ⅛", ⁵⁄₁₆", and 1" circle punches
- ⅞" bow punch

For the Ferocious Lion:

- Orange, tan, black, and white foam
- 3" of orange 6-mm chenille
- Black thread
- ⅛", ⁵⁄₁₆", and 1" circle punches
- Decorative scissors

For the Smiley Frog:

- Green and black foam
- 2 green ⅝" and 2 yellow ⁷⁄₁₆" precut circles
- 3" of green 3-mm chenille
- Red marker
- ⅛", ⁵⁄₁₆", and 1" circle punches

For the Joyful Snowman:

- White, black, red, blue, and orange foam
- 3" of white 6-mm chenille
- Black marker
- ¼", ⁵⁄₁₆", and 1" circle punches
- Decorative scissors

For the Festive Reindeer:

- Tan, brown, white, red, and black foam
- 3" of brown 6-mm chenille
- 3" of red crochet thread
- ⅛", ⁵⁄₁₆", and 1" circle punches
- 3-mm bell

For the Beatific Angel:

- White, brown, yellow, red, and tan foam
- 3" of white 3-mm chenille
- ⁵⁄₁₆", 1", and 1¼" circle punches
- ⅞" bow punch
- Decorative scissors

TIPS: Use 1" punch to cut the face and halo. • Punch a 1¼" brown circle for the hair. • Cut out the hair with decorative scissors.

For Jolly Santa:

- Red, white, black, tan, green, and yellow foam
- 3" of red 3-mm chenille
- ⅛", ¼", ⁵⁄₁₆", and 1" circle punches
- 1¼" heart punch
- Decorative scissors

TIPS: Cut a ¼" x 3" strip of black foam for the belt. • To make the beard, punch a 1¼" white heart. • Cut out the heart with decorative scissors.

For the Bow-Tied Bear:

- Brown, tan, red, black, and blue foam
- 2 (⅜") blue precut foam hearts
- 3" of brown 6-mm chenille
- ⅛", ¼", ⁵⁄₁₆", and 1" circle punches

Note: See page 86 for the templates.

1. Transfer the template to the foam and cut out the body. Fold the body into a tube (A). Overlap and glue the back seam.

2. Thread 3" of chenille through the body. Glue the front of the neck to the back of the neck. Punch out four ⁵⁄₁₆" circles for hands. On each end of the chenille, glue the circles together, sandwiching the chenille end (B).

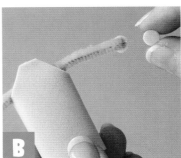

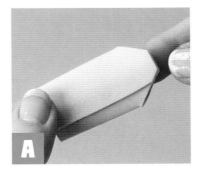

3. Punch out the 1" circle for the head. Glue on the facial features or draw the face with markers. Glue the head to the neck (C).

4. Glue the ears to the back of the head (D). Finish the puppet with the remaining pattern pieces.

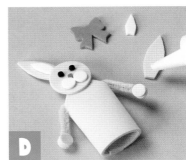

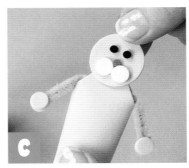

More Finger Puppet Fun! Templates

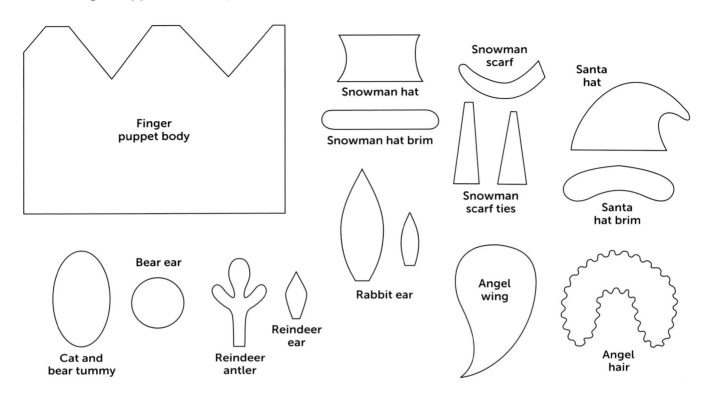

Finger puppet body

Snowman hat

Snowman hat brim

Snowman scarf

Snowman scarf ties

Santa hat

Santa hat brim

Rabbit ear

Angel wing

Angel hair

Bear ear

Cat and bear tummy

Reindeer antler

Reindeer ear

Terrific Balancers Templates (copy at 200%)

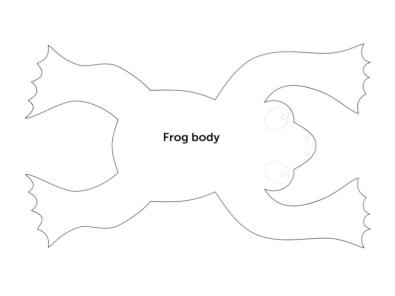

Frog body

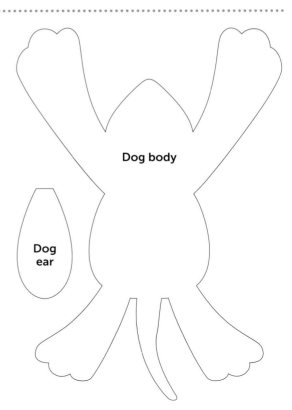

Dog body

Dog ear

TERRIFIC BALANCERS

If you find the right spot, you can balance these animals on the end of a pencil, your finger, or other small point, and they will stay steady. Have fun impressing your friends and family with this great juggling act!

For the Spotted Frog:

- Green, lime green, and black foam
- 2 (⁷⁄₁₆") yellow precut foam circles
- 2 washers or pennies
- Dark green marker
- ⅛", ¼", and ⁵⁄₁₆" circle punches
- 9" of ¼" dowel, optional
- 1 (1½") wood wheel, optional

For the Floppy Dog:

- Tan, brown, black, and red foam
- 1 (¾") white precut foam heart
- Brown and red watercolor markers
- 2 washers or pennies
- ¼" and ⁵⁄₁₆" circle punches
- 9" of ¼" dowel, optional
- 1 (1½") wood wheel, optional

A

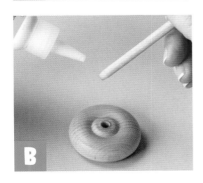

B

1. Transfer the pattern to the foam. Cut out the shapes. Shade the edges of the foam with the markers (green for the frog; brown for the dog).

2. Glue the shapes together. Glue the washers under the tips of the wings (A). If the critter does not balance well, move the weight forward or add more weight to the wings.

3. Glue 9" of the ¼" dowel into center of 1½" wood wheel (B). Balance the critter on the dowel, the tip of your finger, or your nose. Run relay races with a group or time how long you can walk and balance your critter at the same time.

EYE MASKS

Foam is a great medium for your next Halloween costume or school play. With a little imagination, your options are limitless!

For the Charming Cow:

- Cow print, black, and tan foam
- Brown and pink watercolor markers
- 18" of black round elastic cord
- 2 (½") white buttons
- ⅛" circle punch

TIP: Cut out the ear from the tiger ear pattern and fold in half.

For the Red-Nosed Reindeer:

- Tan, brown, and white foam
- 1 (1¼") red precut foam circle
- Brown watercolor marker
- 18" of black round elastic cord
- 2 (½") tan buttons
- Decorative scissors
- ⅛" circle punch

TIP: The nose can be cut out with a 1¼" circle punch.

For the Fierce Tiger:

- Tiger print, black, and white foam
- 18" of black round elastic cord
- 2 (½") orange buttons
- Zigzag scissors
- ⅛" circle punch

TIP: Cut ⅛" strips of black foam to make whiskers.
Note: See page 90 for the templates.

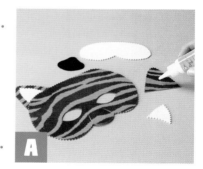

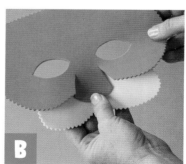

1. Transfer the templates to the foam and cut out the shapes. Cut out the eyeholes. Glue on the ears and horns (A).

2. To make room for your nose, cut and spread slashes beside the nose and glue to the muzzle (B).

3. Punch out holes in the side of the mask. Tie a knot in one end of the elastic (C). Put glue on the knot to secure. Thread a button on the elastic and then thread the elastic through the hole in the mask from the wrong side. Wrap the elastic over the side of mask and across the back. Thread the elastic through the second hole from the front, add the button, and tie the knot in the end of the elastic. Dot the knot with glue.

Eye Masks Templates

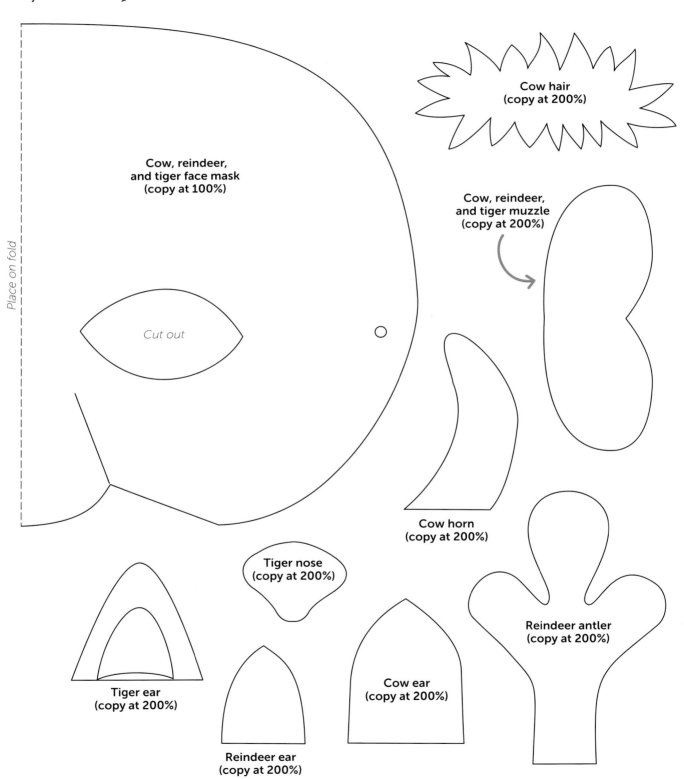

Place on fold

Cow, reindeer,
and tiger face mask
(copy at 100%)

Cut out

Cow hair
(copy at 200%)

Cow, reindeer,
and tiger muzzle
(copy at 200%)

Cow horn
(copy at 200%)

Tiger nose
(copy at 200%)

Reindeer antler
(copy at 200%)

Tiger ear
(copy at 200%)

Reindeer ear
(copy at 200%)

Cow ear
(copy at 200%)

SILLY BIRD MASK

This is great for birthday parties, Halloween, and the first day of spring! It looks especially good with a yellow shirt, yellow pants, and orange socks.

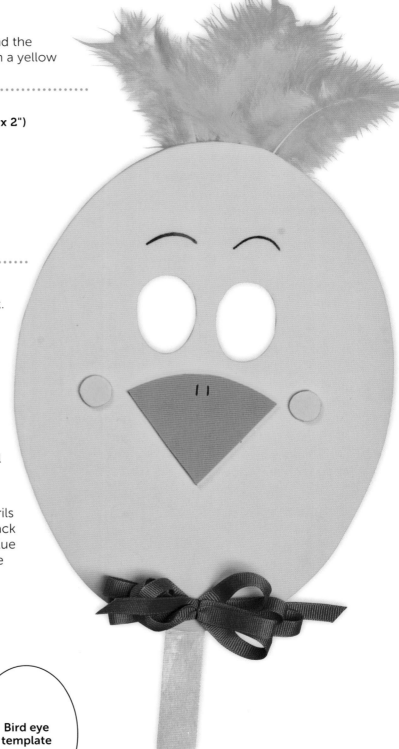

- ● Craft foam (9" x 12" sheets):
  - ■ 1 yellow (cut 1 basic mask and 1 piece 1" x 2")
  - ■ 1 orange (cut 1 bird beak)
  - ■ 1 pink (cut 2 bird cheeks)
- ● ¼"-wide green grosgrain ribbon, 24" long
- ● 1 (3½" x 3½") piece of cardboard
- ● 3" floral wire
- ● Wood tongue depressor
- ● 3 yellow boa feathers

Note: See page 97 for the basic mask template.

1. Cut out the bird eye openings in the mask. Glue the beak and cheeks to the mask.

2. Wrap the ribbon around the cardboard, slide it off carefully, and secure it tightly in the center with floral wire to make a bow. Poke the wire into the mask ½" from the lower edge. Bend the wire up and secure in the back with a dot of glue.

3. Glue a tongue depressor onto the back of the mask, being sure to cover the floral wire piece.

4. Use a fine-tip marker to add an eyebrow above each eye and two ¼" lines for nostrils on the beak. Glue three feathers to the back of the mask so they stick up at the top. Glue the small piece of yellow foam behind the feathers to secure them.

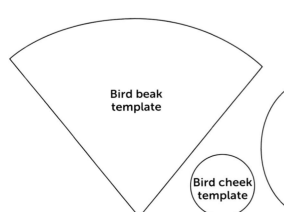

Bird beak template

Bird cheek template

Bird eye template

HAUGHTY PRINCESS MASK

With this mask you can be Queen or Princess of any land you can imagine, or the star of a Mardi Gras party! Don't forget to be kind to your subjects!

- Craft foam (9" x 12" sheets):
  - 1 pink (cut 1 basic mask and 1 princess nose)
  - 1 pink glitter (cut 2 princess cheeks)
  - 1 yellow (cut 1 princess hair)
  - 1 dark pink (cut 1 princess lips)
  - 1 gold glitter (cut 1 princess crown)
- Wood tongue depressor
- Assorted rhinestones

Note: See pages 96–97 for the templates.

1. Trace and cut out the basic mask template from the foam. Cut out the princess eye openings in the mask. Glue the hair, nose, cheeks, and lips to the mask. Glue the crown to the hair.

2. Glue the rhinestones to the crown as desired. Glue on various rhinestone shapes to the crown.

3. Use a fine-tip marker to add all lines on the mask, hair, and lips.

4. Glue the tongue depressor to the bottom of the mask, leaving 3" showing.

PUPPY DOG MASK

Team up with a friend in the kitten mask, or do your own puppy thing. Put the bow under the chin for a boy dog or at the top of the head for a girl dog.

- Craft foam (9" x 12" sheets):
  - 1 tan (cut 1 basic mask)
  - 1 brown (cut 2 dog ears)
  - 1 ivory (cut 1 dog muzzle)
  - 1 black (cut 1 dog nose)
- ¼" purple gingham checked ribbon, 20" long
- 1 (2¾" x 2¾") piece of cardboard
- 1 (2½") piece of floral wire
- Wood tongue depressor
- Acrylic paint: titanium white and lamp black

Note: See pages 96–97 for the templates.

1. Trace and cut out the basic mask template from the foam. Cut out the dog eye openings in the mask. Glue the ears and mouth to the mask. Glue the nose to the muzzle.

2. Paint all details on the muzzle and eyebrows lamp black. Use lamp black and a stylus to add dots to the muzzle. Paint the nose line titanium white.

3. Wrap the ribbon around the cardboard, carefully slide it off, and secure it tightly in the center with floral wire to make a bow.

4. Poke floral wire into the top side of the mask. Bend the wire to be flat against head. Glue on a small piece of tan craft foam to cover the wire.

5. Glue a tongue depressor to the bottom of the mask, leaving at least 3" showing.

LOVELY CAT MASK

Expect to hear lots of awwws as you meow your way into people's hearts! Wear a fuzzy gray sweater, gray pants, black socks, and black mittens to complete this costume.

- **Craft foam (9" x 12" sheets):**
  - 1 gray (cut 1 cat mask and 2 cat ears)
  - 1 pink (cut 1 tongue and 2 cat ear centers)
  - 1 black (cut 1 cat nose)
- **6 black chenille stems**
- **⅜" pink grosgrain ribbon, 8" long**
- **Wood tongue depressor**
- **Acrylic paint: titanium white and lamp black**

Note: See page 95 for the templates.

1. Trace and cut out the basic mask template from the foam. Cut out the cat eye openings in the mask. Paint a small titanium white square on the nose. Paint all details on the mask and the center of the ears lamp black.

2. Glue pink centers to the center of the gray ears and glue the ears onto top of the mask. Glue the tongue into the point of the mouth.

3. Use needle-nose pliers to cut each chenille stem approximately 3½" long and glue them onto the mask for whiskers.

4. Tie a bow with the ribbon and glue it between the ears at the top of the mask.

5. Glue a tongue depressor to the bottom of the mask, leaving at least 3" showing.

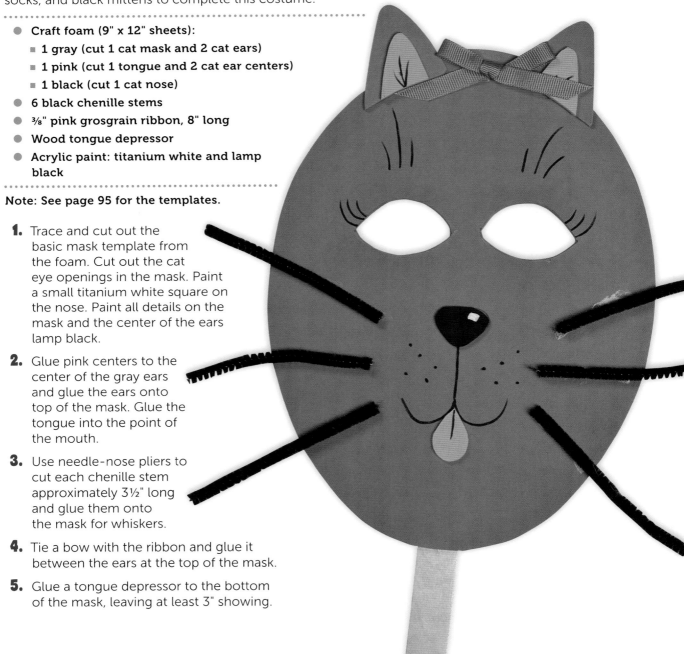

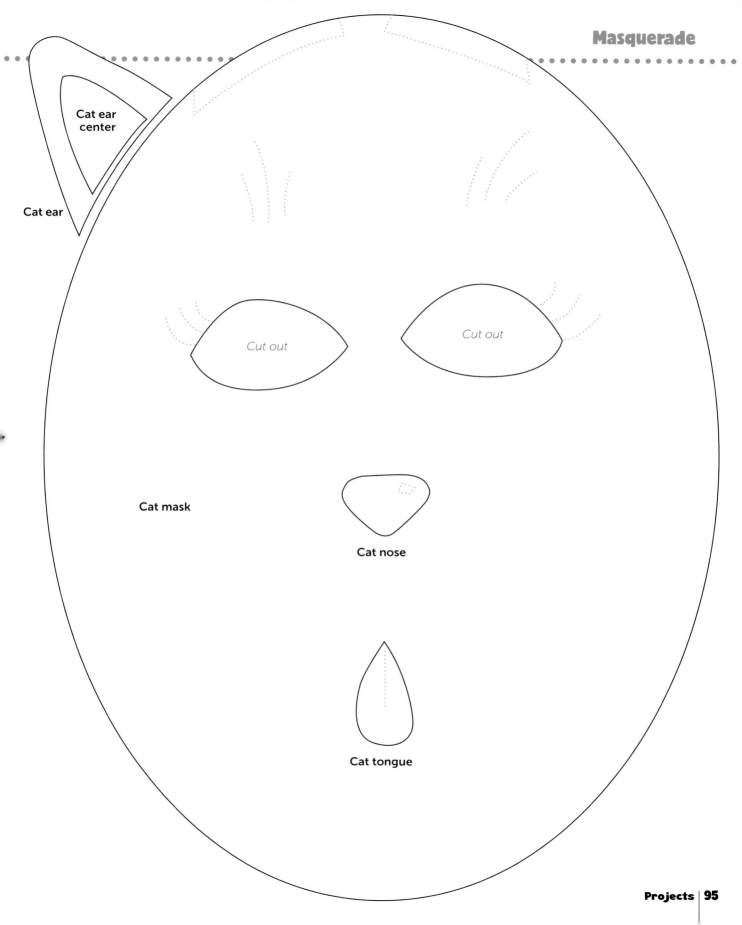

Cat ear center

Cat ear

Cut out

Cut out

Cat mask

Cat nose

Cat tongue

Haughty Princess Mask Templates (copy at 200%)

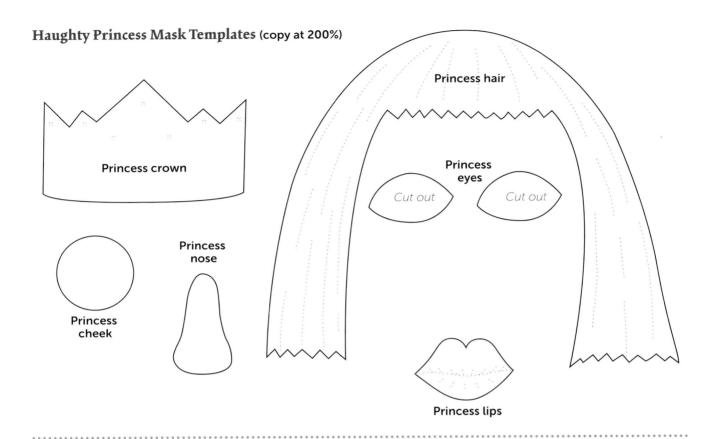

Princess crown

Princess hair

Princess eyes

Cut out   *Cut out*

Princess nose

Princess cheek

Princess lips

Puppy Dog Mask Templates (copy at 200%)

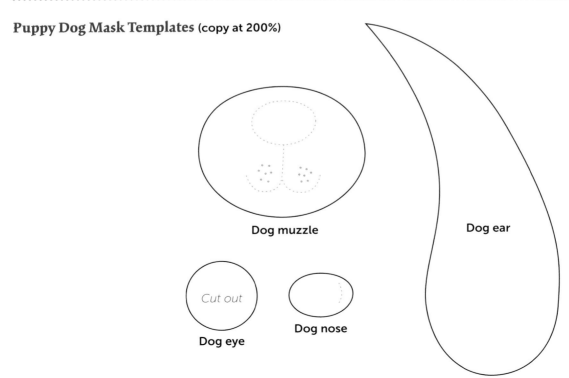

Dog muzzle

Dog ear

Cut out

Dog eye

Dog nose

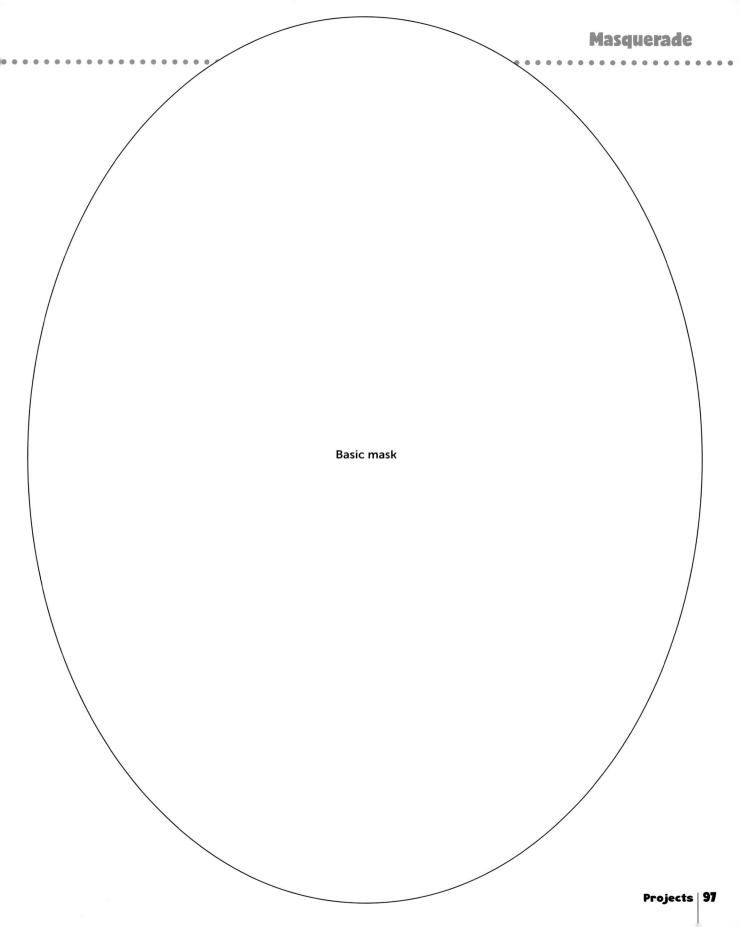

Basic mask

SHINY STAR NECKLACE

This stylish necklace is easy to make. Combine it with any of the other star projects in this section for a truly dazzling look, perfect for any star!

- 1 (9" x 12" sheet) gold glitter craft foam (cut 1 star A)
- 24" of ¹⁄₁₆" lilac sparkly silky cord

1. Use a hole punch to make a hole in two star points vertically across from each other.

2. Thread the cording through from back of the star. Tie a knot at end of cording.

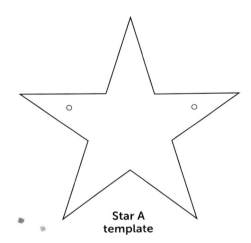

Star A
template

STAR POWER BRACELET

Accessorize your wardrobe with this bracelet! Use the stars, as shown, or substitute hearts, butterflies, or some other shape.

- Craft foam (9" x 12" sheets):
  - 1 gold glitter (cut 5 or 6 star B's)
  - 1 green glitter (cut 2 star C's)
  - 1 purple (cut 1 star C)
- Gold metallic chenille stem or wired gold metallic tinsel/cording (length depends on size of wrist)

1. Measure your wrist and cut chenille, tinsel, or cording 1" longer than that. Twist the ends together to form a circle, making sure the bracelet is not too tight.

2. Glue stars onto the circle and use clothespins until dry.

DOUBLE STAR RING

The magical powers of this ring are available only to the one who wears it. Be gone and create!

- Craft foam (9" x 12" sheets):
- 1 purple glitter (cut 1 star C)
- 1 gold glitter (cut 1 star B)
- Gold metallic chenille stem or wired tinsel/cording

1. Cut a chenille stem or wired tinsel/cording to fit your finger with some overlap to twist together. Bend the twisted end to flatten it against the ring.

2. Glue a gold star onto a purple star at an angle. Glue the purple star over the twisted area of the ring and use clothespins until dry.

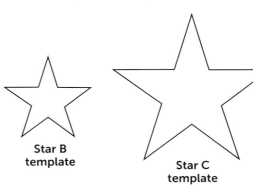

Star B
template

Star C
template

MAGICAL STAR WAND

Next time you take a walk, use this wand to touch a leaf or flower and save a fairy. Pay close attention and maybe you'll see a fairy, small animal, or other fun surprise!

- 1 (9" x 12" sheet) gold glitter craft foam (cut 2 star A's)
- Drinking straw
- ⅛" grosgrain ribbon, 18" long: orange satin, yellow satin, pink satin, and purple

1. Glue a straw between the backs of two stars.

2. Tie ribbons onto the straw.

ROYAL CROWN

King, queen, prince, or princess—this crown is fit for them all. Make one for each member of your family and let them choose which gems they want.

- 1 (9" x 12" sheet) gold glitter craft foam (cut 1 crown and 1 star B)
- 3½" strip of hook-and-loop tape
- Various styles of rhinestones, buttons, and bows

1. Cut a 1¾" x 10" strip from gold glitter foam and glue to one side of the crown. Use clothespins until dry. On the other end, glue one section of hook-and-loop tape.

2. Glue the remaining section of the hook-and-loop tape to the crown. This will help determine the size needed to fit the wearer.

3. Glue the star to the top of the center point.

4. Glue on rhinestones, buttons, and bows as desired.

Wand and Crown Templates

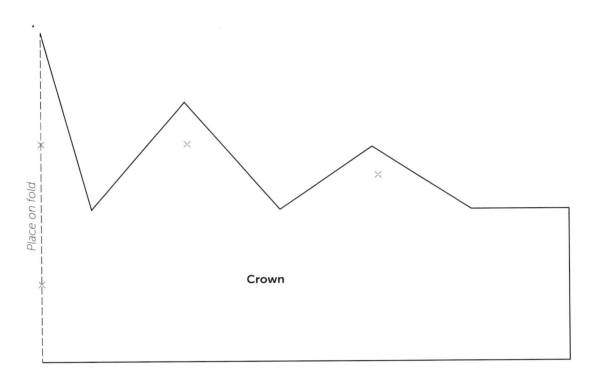

Place on fold

Crown

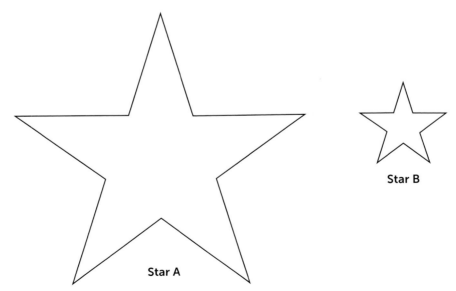

Star A

Star B

BOUNCY HEADBAND BOBBERS

These festive headbands make great party hats and holiday costumes!
They're super cool and will have everyone's head turning.

For the Springtime Butterflies:

- Yellow foam
- Precut foam hearts:
  - 4 (⅜") yellow
  - 4 (¾") magenta
  - 4 (1¼") purple
- Purple plastic headband
- 48" of black wire
- 2 small nails
- 2 black spaghetti beads
- 2 black 4-mm beads
- Decorative scissors

TIPS: The purple heart can be cut with 1¼" heart punch. • Bend 3" of
wire in half. • Loosely coil the wire ends to form antennae. • Thread the
beads onto the antennae. • Glue the uncoiled portion of coiled wire into a
spaghetti bead. • Glue magenta hearts to purple hearts. • Cut straight across
the points of hearts. • Glue the wings to the body. • Use decorative scissors
to cut ¼" strips of yellow foam. • Glue to the headband.

For the Wintery Snowflakes:

- White foam
- 7 white precut foam flowers
- White plastic headband
- 2 small nails
- 48" of white wire
- Blue marker
- ⅛" diamond punch

TIPS: Punch two diamonds in each arm of the large snowflake.
• Punch one diamond in the petals of the flowers.

Snowflake template

For the Lovely Hearts:

- Pink foam
- Precut foam hearts:
  - 2 (¾") red
  - 2 (1⅝") red
  - 2 (1¼") pink
- Red plastic headband
- 48" of red wire
- 2 small nails
- Decorative scissors

TIP: After attaching bobbers, use scissors to cut ⅜" strips of pink foam and glue to the headband.

1. **This step should be done by an adult:** Mark two dots 4" apart on top of the plastic headband. Working from the inside of the headband, hammer a small nail through each dot (A). Cut the nails off, leaving ½" showing on top of the headband. File the nails down smooth.

2. Wrap two 24" pieces of wire on a meat skewer, leaving 1" of wire uncoiled on one end. Remove from the skewer and stretch the coils slightly (B).

3. Glue two shapes together, placing the straight end of a coiled wire between the shapes (C). Glue a coil over the nail. Cut and glue the foam strips or shapes to the headband.

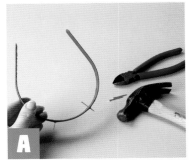
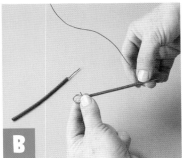
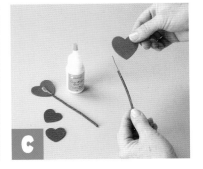

CRAFTY BRACELETS

Change up your foam colors, decorative scissors, and embellishments for an endless supply of bracelets!

- **Craft thread**
- **Adhesive-backed craft and glitter foam, 1"- and 1¼"-wide strips**
- **Zigzag scissors**
- **Size 18 needlepoint needle (does not have sharp point)**
- **½" buttons**
- **Flat-back crystals**
- **⅛" circle hole punch**
- **Small ribbon slot punch**

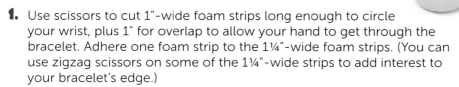

1. Use scissors to cut 1"-wide foam strips long enough to circle your wrist, plus 1" for overlap to allow your hand to get through the bracelet. Adhere one foam strip to the 1¼"-wide foam strips. (You can use zigzag scissors on some of the 1¼"-wide strips to add interest to your bracelet's edge.)

2. Glue the buttons in place. Punch holes around the buttons. Sew around, through, and over the buttons.

3. Stitch the thread circles. Make stitches from the back into the center of the circle and clip threads to make a fringe.

4. Punch out more holes. Sew stitches through the holes.

5. Overlap the ends and sew the pieces together with long stitches.

HEART-SHAPED GLASSES

These funny love specs are so fun to wear! See if guests at your Valentine party can tell who you are behind them.

- Craft foam (9" x 12" sheets):
  - 1 red (cut 2 heart A's and 1 piece ⅜" x 1½")
  - 1 white (cut 2 heart C's)
  - 1 pink (cut 2 heart B's)
- 2 gold metallic chenille stems
- Ice crystal glitter paint
- Foam or dimensional paint: white, hot pink, and red

1. Trace and cut out all shapes from the appropriate foam colors.

2. Cut out the centers of the red hearts. Use foam or dimensional paint to outline the large hearts with white and hot pink, the white hearts with hot pink, and the red hearts with red. Apply ice crystal glitter paint to all of the hearts. Glue the hearts together as shown.

3. Use a hole punch to make a hole to insert the chenille stems.

4. Glue a strip of red foam between the two large hearts for the nosepiece; measure between your eyes to have enough space between the hearts and fit comfortably on the bridge of your nose. Push the chenille stem through the hole from the back and curl a couple times around a pencil to keep the earpiece from pulling out. Bend the end of the chenille stem to form over your ear.

VALENTINE CARD

Everyone loves to get a Valentine card, especially if the sender made the card personally! This clever card has an added treat.

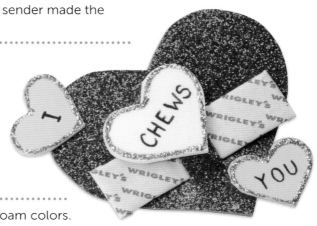

- Craft foam (9" x 12" sheets):
  - 1 fuchsia glitter (cut 1 of heart A)
  - 1 pink (cut 2 heart D's)
  - 1 white (cut 1 heart B)
- 1 stick of chewing gum
- 1 (3⅝" x 6½") envelope
- Lamp black acrylic paint
- Gold glitter dimensional paint

1. Trace and cut out all shapes from the appropriate foam colors.

2. Paint the lettering lamp black. Use gold glitter to outline the white and pink hearts.

3. Use a knife to cut two slits onto the glitter heart. Slip a stick of chewing gum into the slit.

4. Glue the pink and white hearts to the glitter heart.

VALENTINE BIRDIE BOX

Valentines are even more fun when you have a special box to keep them in. This box is big enough that it might hold several years' worth of valentines!

- ● Craft foam (9" x 12" sheets):
  - ■ 1 (12" x 18" sheet) white (will cover almost any size tissue box)
  - ■ 1 light pink (cut 8 heart B's)
  - ■ 1 (12" x 18" sheet) pink (cut 1 head, 2 heart A's, and 10 heart B's)
  - ■ 1 white (cut 2 heart B's)
  - ■ 1 yellow (cut 2 beaks)
  - ■ 1 red (cut 2 heart D's)
- ● 2 (¼") wiggle eyes
- ● Empty box of facial tissues
- ● 3 pink boa feathers
- ● 3 pink chenille stems (cut into five 4"-long pieces)
- ● Decorative trim—measure around tissue box to determine amount needed

1. Cut foam to fit a tissue box and glue it on. Trace and cut out all other shapes from the appropriate foam colors.

2. Glue a light pink heart to the end of each stem. Twist the stems and feathers together into a tail and glue it to the box. Glue one large pink heart over the tail chenille ends. Glue on eyes and beaks. Use a fine-tip marker to draw eyebrows.

3. Glue three light pink hearts to the head and neck. Use a knife to lightly score (cut partway through the foam) ¼" from the neck edge. Fold along the scored line and glue to the box.

4. To support the head, cut a ¼" x 4" white craft foam strip to glue on the opposite side of the fold. Lightly score ¼" from the large pink heart points.

5. Glue the red and white hearts to the large pink heart. Glue the score line on both hearts to the sides of the box. Adhere trim to the top edge of the box.

Valentine Craft Templates

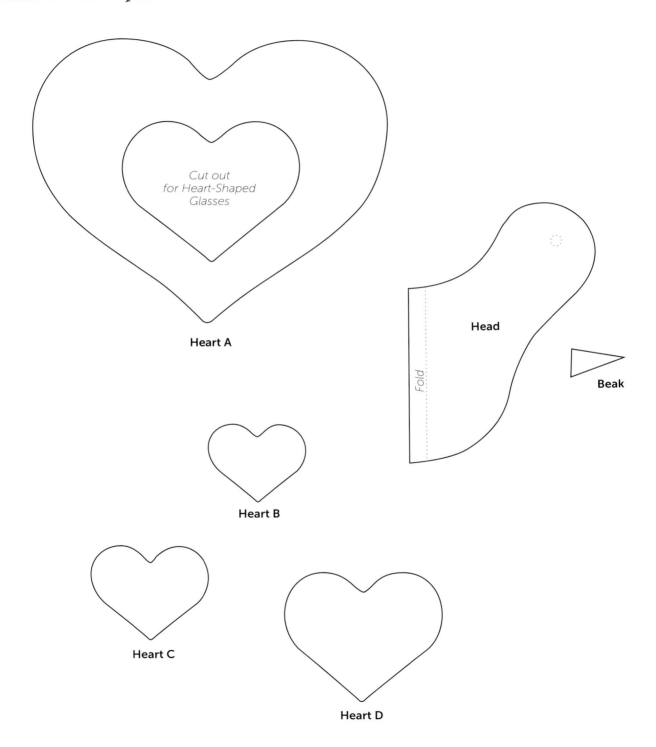

*Cut out
for Heart-Shaped
Glasses*

Heart A

Head

Fold

Beak

Heart B

Heart C

Heart D

EASTER BUNNY BASKET

This is an easy way to decorate a plain basket for Easter. Just add Easter grass and fill it with candy or cookies for dessert.

- **Craft foam (9" x 12" sheets):**
  - 1 white (cut 6 bunny heads and 12 bunny ears)
  - 1 pink (cut 12 bunny inner ears)
  - 1 gray (punch 6 circles ¼")
- **¼"-wide satin picot ribbon:**
  - 1¼ yard yellow
  - 1½ yard mint green
  - 1¼ yard purple
- **1 (4" x 5") piece of cardboard**
- **Basket (approximately 4" x 6" x 8")**
- **12 (³⁄₁₆") wiggle eyes**
- **Lamp black acrylic paint**

1. Trace and cut out all shapes from the appropriate foam colors.

2. Glue gray circles onto the heads as noses. Glue wiggle eyes above the nose.

3. Paint a ¼" lamp black line down from each nose and eyebrows above each eye. Glue the pink centers to each ear. Glue two ears to each head.

4. Use 6" of each picot ribbon color to make a bow and glue it between the ears. Glue rabbits evenly around the basket.

5. Cut a 6" piece of mint green ribbon. Wrap remaining ribbons around the cardboard, slide it off carefully, and use the green ribbon to secure it tightly in the center, creating a bow. Tie onto the center of the basket handle.

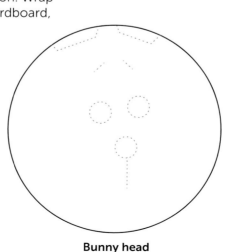

Bunny head template

Bunny ear template

Bunny inner ear template

EASTER EGG HOLDER

This Easter egg in its own holder is the perfect decoration or gift to celebrate the holiday. Make it even more special by writing the year and each person's name on his or her egg.

- Craft foam (9" x 12" sheets):
  - 1 white (cut 1¼" x 6¾")
  - 1 yellow (cut ⅜" x 6¾")
- Scrap pieces of pink, lavender, and light green foam (each at least 1" x 1")
- 1 (2½") wood egg (or use a real hard-boiled egg)
- Acrylic paint: bubblegum pink, marigold, purple cow, sour apple, and titanium white

1. Measure your egg to be sure you have enough white and yellow craft foam for the egg stand.

2. Use a large hole punch to make ¼" circles from the scrap pieces of craft foam in various colors.

3. Glue the punched circles onto the yellow strip. Glue the yellow strip to the center of the white strip.

4. Overlap ½" and glue the ends together to form a circle. Before the glue dries, make sure the egg will sit in the stand. Use clothespins until dry.

5. Paint the egg titanium white. It may take three to four coats; let it dry completely between each coat.

6. Use a pencil to draw a ⅝" strip vertically around the egg. Paint the strip marigold. Again, it may take several coats.

7. Dot bubblegum pink, purple cow, and sour apple onto the strip.

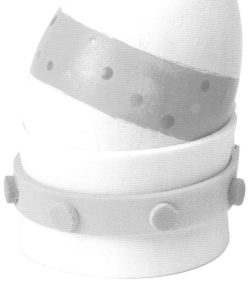

SUMMERTIME LADYBUG PLACEMAT

Bring ladybugs and dragonflies to the table on this fun placemat. Make enough for all your guests at a barbecue or picnic.

- **Craft foam (9" x 12" sheets):**
  - **1 white (cut 6 dragonfly wings)**
  - **1 black (cut 6 thoraxes, 1 ladybug head, 3 ladybug spots, and 1 ladybug stripe)**
  - **1 red (cut 1 ladybug body)**
- **1 (12" x 18") green craft foam sheet**
- **Ice crystal glitter paint**
- **Sour apple acrylic paint**
- **3½" of 18 gauge copper wire**

1. Trace and cut out all shapes from the appropriate foam colors.

2. Apply ice crystal glitter paint onto the dragonfly.

3. Dot sour apple eyes onto the thorax. Glue the thorax on top of the dragonfly.

4. Use needle-nose pliers to bend the copper wire into a U-shape. Poke one end of wire into the top of the head. Bend the ends into a circle.

5. Glue the ladybug head, stripe, and dots to body. Glue the ladybug to the center of the placemat.

6. Glue three dragonflies to each side of the placemat.

Ladybug Placemat Templates

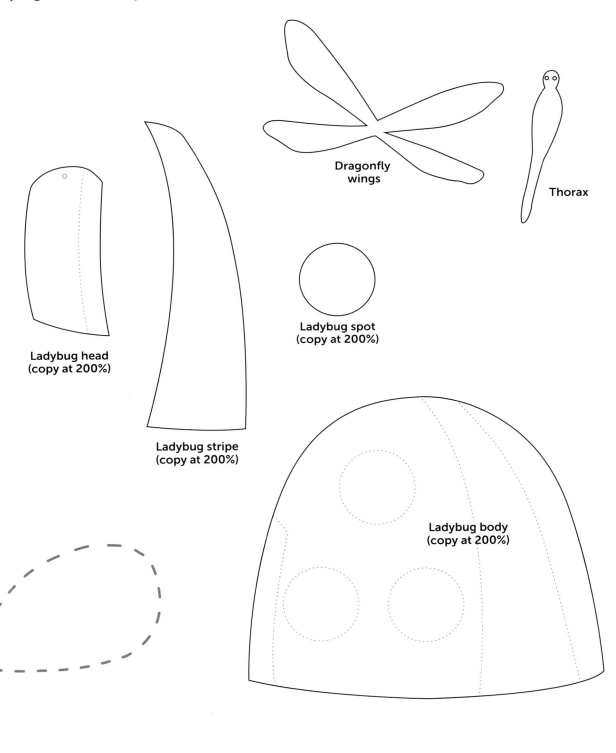

Dragonfly
wings

Thorax

Ladybug head
(copy at 200%)

Ladybug spot
(copy at 200%)

Ladybug stripe
(copy at 200%)

Ladybug body
(copy at 200%)

DRAGONFLY CUP HOLDER

This cup holder can be made to fit any cup size. It's easy to personalize the holder by writing a name on it.

- **Craft foam (9" x 12" sheets):**
  - 1 lavender (measure around glass/cup for size)
  - 1 white (cut 4 dragonfly wings)
  - 1 black (cut 4 thoraxes)
- **Sour apple acrylic paint**
- **Ice crystal glitter paint**

1. Trace and cut out all shapes from the appropriate foam colors.

2. Dot sour apple eyes onto each thorax.

3. Apply ice crystal glitter paint to the entire wing surface.

4. Glue the thorax on top of the wings.

5. Glue the dragonflies onto the cup holder.

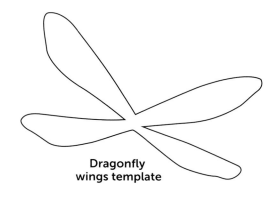

Dragonfly
wings template

Thorax
template

PATRIOTIC FIRECRACKER HAT

This fits-any-size hat is just the thing to celebrate the 4th of July, Veteran's Day, or any holiday that could use some sparkle and pizzazz. If you don't live in the United States, just adjust the colors and lettering to reflect your own country.

- Craft foam (9" x 12" sheets):
  - 1 white (cut 1 candle)
  - 1 red (cut 1 candle and 1 star)
  - 1 blue (cut 1 candle and 1 star)
- 1 (12" x 18") black foam sheet (1¼" x measurement around head of wearer)
- 3 gold metallic 1½" chenille stems
- Gold glitter dimensional paint
- 3 (1¼") glitter pom-poms
- 1⅛" glitter sticker letters
- 3 (2½") wooden craft sticks
- Acrylic paint: cherry red, ocean blue, and titanium white

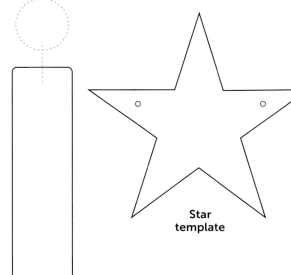

Star template

Candle template

1. Slightly round the corners of three candles. Glue on chenille stems. Glue glitter pom-poms onto the stems.

2. Paint one wooden craft stick cherry red, one ocean blue, and one titanium white. When dry, glue to the back of the candles.

3. Glue the ends of the hatband together. Use clothespins until dry.

4. Glue firecrackers to the front of the headband. Press on glitter letters.

5. Outline the stars with gold glitter and glue onto the hat.

ROAD PLAY MAT

Use this play mat with cars, trucks, boats, and trains you made yourself or bought. Add more roads, railroads, or ponds if you want by expanding the size of your play mat.

- **Craft foam (12" x 18" sheets):**
  - **4 green**
  - **1 brown (cut 4 strips 3" x 18" for roads)**
- **1 (9" x 12" sheet) blue glitter foam (cut 1 pond)**
- **1 black foam sheet (cut 1 racetrack and many ⁹⁄₁₆" x 12" strips)**
- **Sewing machine with green thread OR green duct tape**

1. Trace and cut out the template pieces from the appropriate foam colors.

2. Sew or tape together four sheets of green foam to create a 24" x 36" mat. Glue brown road strips over the stitching or use duct tape.

3. Trim any excess to make the roads even with the outer edges of the mat.

4. Glue four ⁹⁄₁₆" x 12" strips across the short way 1⅜" apart to form tracks. Cut the remaining strips into 3" rails and glue approximately ¾" apart across the tracks.

5. Glue the pond and racetrack onto the mat.

Road Play Mat Templates

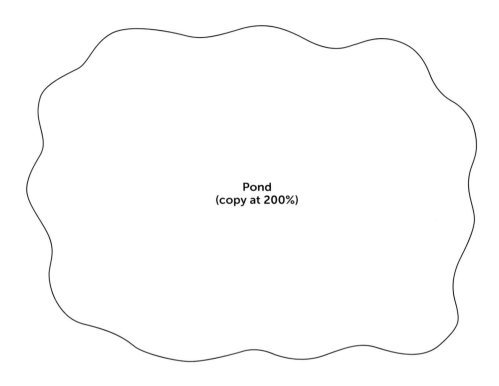

Pond
(copy at 200%)

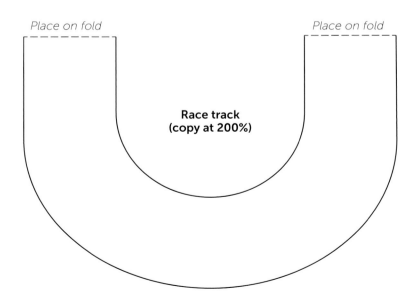

Place on fold   *Place on fold*

Race track
(copy at 200%)

STEAM ENGINE TRAIN & SIGN

Choo-choo! Make your way down the play mat track with this train, and use the railroad crossing sign to make sure everyone knows you're coming!

- **Craft foam (9" x 12" sheets):**
  - 1 black (cut 2 trains and 2 train hubcaps)
  - 1 gray (cut 2 smokestacks)
  - 1 tan (cut 2 pieces ¼" x 1¾", for roofs; cut 2 cow catchers)
  - 1 yellow (cut 2 lights)
  - 1 brown (cut 4 train wheels)
  - 1 white (cut 2 pieces ½" x 2", for sign)
- **2 (½" x ½") wood blocks**
- **2" wood axle**
- **1 (1⅛") wood spool**
- **Lamp black acrylic paint**
- **Fine-tip marker**
- **Broad-tip marker**

1. Trace and cut out the template pieces from the appropriate foam colors.

2. Paint the wood blocks, wood axle, and wood spool lamp black.

3. Use a fine-tip marker to print "Crossing" on one white strip. Glue two white strips together in an X, with "Crossing" on top.

4. Print "Railroad" on the back strip.

5. Use a broad-tip marker to add lines to the cow catcher.

6. On each side, glue on the train roof, smoke stack, cow catcher, and light. Glue a black wood block between the bodies so the train stands. Glue the hubcaps to the wheels and the wheels to the train body. Make sure they are even so the train stands upright. Glue the axle into the hole of the spool. Glue the railroad sign to the axle.

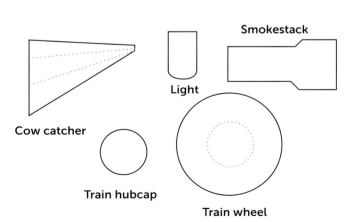

Cow catcher

Light

Smokestack

Train hubcap

Train wheel

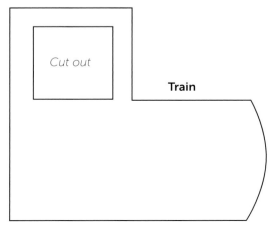

Cut out

Train

MOVING TRUCK

It's moving day for the play mat neighborhood, and this helpful vehicle has everything under control.

- **Craft foam (9" x 12" sheets):**
  - **1 gray (cut 2 truck sides)**
  - **1 black (cut 6 wheels)**
  - **1 chartreuse green (cut 2 truck cabs and 2 moving bumpers)**
  - **1 blue (cut 4 hubcaps)**
  - **1 yellow (cut 2 moving headlights)**
- **1⅛" foam glitter adhesive-backed letters**
- **2 (½" x ½") wood blocks**
- **Acrylic paint: slate gray, lamp black, and sour apple**

1. Trace and cut out the template pieces from the appropriate foam colors.

2. Paint lamp black lines on the truck cab and "Moving" (and your name, if desired, in foam letters) onto the truck box area. Paint one wood block slate gray and one sour apple.

3. Adhere the foam letters to the truck box area. Glue the truck cab to the box. Glue the sour apple block between the cab and slate gray block between the box sections so the truck will stand.

4. Glue the hubcaps to the wheels. Glue the wheels to the truck, making sure they are even so the truck will stand upright. Glue the headlights to the front of the truck. Glue the bumpers to the rear of the truck.

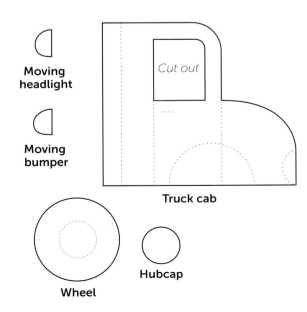

Moving headlight

Moving bumper

Wheel

Hubcap

Truck cab

Cut out

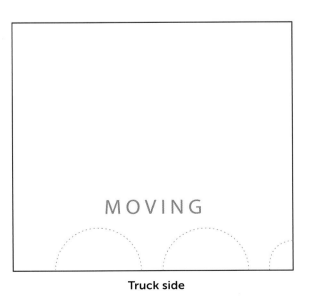

MOVING

Truck side

ZOOMING RACE CAR

The racetrack is perfect for the race car, but if you want to vrooooooom your way around the neighborhood, this race car is the vehicle for you.

- **Craft foam (9" x 12" sheets):**
  - **1 yellow (cut 2 race cars)**
  - **1 black (cut 4 wheels and 1 seat)**
  - **1 orange (cut 4 hubcaps)**
- **2 (½" x ½") wood blocks**
- **Yellow light acrylic paint**
- **Calypso blue dimensional paint**

1. Trace and cut out the template pieces from the appropriate foam colors.

2. Paint both blocks yellow light.

3. Glue the seat to each car body. Glue the blocks between the bodies so the car stands. Glue the hubcaps to the wheels. Glue two wheels to each side of the car body. Make sure they are even so it will stand upright.

4. Use dimensional paint to add a racing stripe and your favorite number. (If you don't have a favorite number, use your age!)

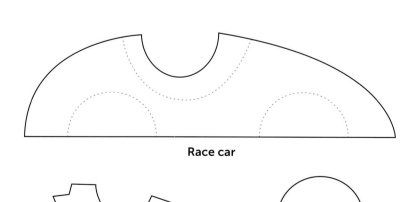

Race car

Seat   Hub cap   Wheel

CLASSIC CAR

Hop your imagination into this car and zip around on the roads of the play mat. Who knows where your journey will end?

- **Craft foam (9" x 12" sheets):**
  - **1 red (cut 2 cars)**
  - **1 yellow (cut 2 headlights)**
  - **1 orange (cut 2 taillights)**
  - **1 gray (cut 4 bumpers)**
  - **1 black (cut 4 wheels)**
- **Ruler**
- **Fine-tip marker**
- **4 (¼") white buttons**
- **4 (⅜") red buttons**
- **2 (½" x ½") wood blocks**
- **Cherry red acrylic paint**

1. Trace and cut out the template pieces from the appropriate foam colors.

2. Use a ruler and fine-tip marker to add door lines.

3. Paint both wood blocks cherry red.

4. Glue the taillight, headlight, and bumpers to each car body side. Make sure the sides across from each other line up properly. Glue the painted blocks between the bodies so the car will stand. Glue the wheels onto the car body. Make sure all wheels are even so the car stands upright. Glue on buttons for the door handles and center of wheels.

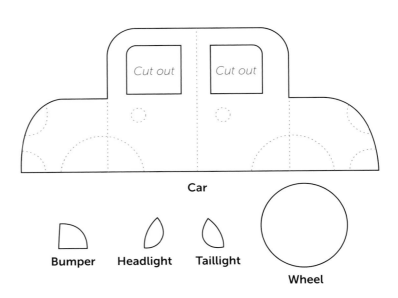

Cut out   Cut out

Car

Bumper   Headlight   Taillight

Wheel

SEAFARING SAILBOAT

Put your name on the side of this boat and sail along on your dreams in the play mat's lake. Better yet, get a friend to make one too and race each other!

- ● Craft foam (9" x 12" sheets):
  - ■ 1 white (cut 1 set of sails)
  - ■ 1 red (cut 1 flag)
  - ■ 1 tan (cut 2 decks)
  - ■ 1 brown (cut 2 hulls)
- ● 6 (¼") black buttons
- ● 1 white drinking straw
- ● Marker

1. Trace and cut out the template pieces from the appropriate foam colors.

2. Glue three buttons onto the top section of the sailboat. Glue the top and bottom sections of the sailboat together.

3. Cut the straw to a length of 5" and glue it to the center of one side of the sailboat. Glue the sails onto the straw ⅝" from the top. Glue the flag to the top of the straw.

4. Glue the remaining side over the straw and glue it to the ends of the sails. Do not glue the ends of the brown section together.

5. Use a marker to add "USA" or your name to side of boat on the brown section.

Sails template

Deck template

Flag template

U S A

Hull template

APPLE TREE

To show a tree in autumn, use red, orange, or yellow instead of green for the leaves and skip the apples. Make more trees of all sizes and colors to create a tree farm.

- **Craft foam (9" x 12" sheets):**
  - **1 green (cut 2 trees)**
  - **1 red, for apples**
  - **1 brown, for the tree trunk**
- **Large hole punch (¼")**
- **Empty toilet paper roll**

1. Trace and cut out the template pieces from the appropriate foam colors.

2. Measure the toilet paper roll and cut the brown craft foam to fit. Glue the foam to the roll, using clothespins until the glue dries.

3. Use a large hole punch to punch ¼" circles out of the red foam and glue them to the green tree section in random spots. Glue the green tree section to the top of the brown tube on both sides. Glue the top of the tree together.

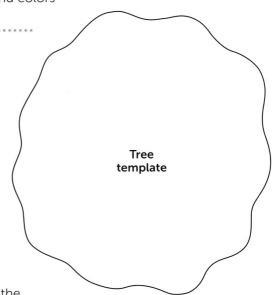

Tree
template

BIG RED BARN

This barn is just the right size for your animals and tractor, and the doors even open so things can pass through.

- Craft foam (9" x 12" sheets):
  - 1 red (cut 1 barn)
  - 1 black (cut 1 barn window)
  - 1 yellow (cut 1 straw)
  - 1 gray (cut 4 hinges)
- 1 white (cut 2 barn doors)
- 1 green (cut 1 barn roof)
- 2 (⅝") black buttons
- 4 (¾" x ¾") wood blocks
- 2 wooden craft sticks
- Cherry red acrylic paint
- Fine-tip black marker
- Ruler

1. Trace and cut out the template pieces from the appropriate foam colors.

2. Paint the blocks and craft sticks cherry red. Use a fine-tip black marker and ruler to draw the straw, board, and wood grain lines.

3. Glue the roof and window to the barn, the straw to the window, the hinges to the barn and doors, and the buttons to the doors. On the back of the barn, glue two blocks on top of each other on each side of the barn doors so it stands by itself. Glue craft sticks above the blocks.

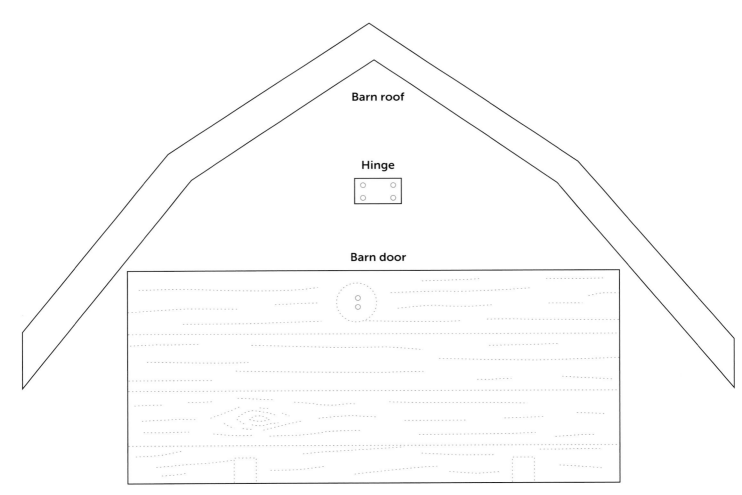

Barn roof

Hinge

Barn door

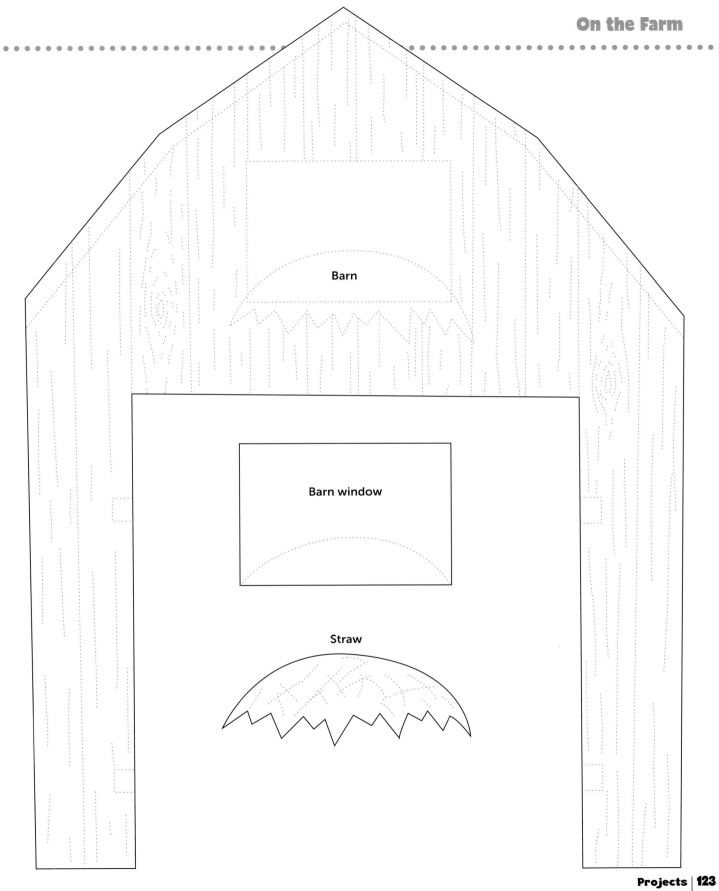

Barn

Barn window

Straw

GREEN TRACTOR

Putt-putt-putt-putt—every farm needs a tractor! Create it in green, red, blue, or your favorite tractor color.

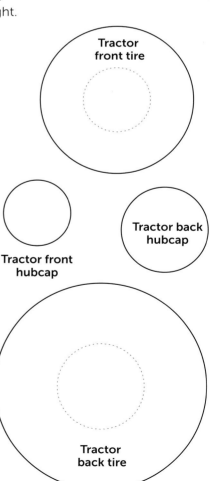

- ● **Craft foam (9" x 12" sheets):**
  - ■ 1 green (cut 2 tractors)
  - ■ 1 yellow (cut 2 each tractor front hubcaps and tractor back hubcaps)
  - ■ 1 black (cut 2 each tractor windows, tractor front tires, and tractor back tires)
- ● **Festive green acrylic paint**
- ● **2 wood blocks ½" x ½"**

1. Trace and cut out the template pieces from the appropriate foam colors.

2. Paint both wood blocks festive green.

3. Glue the wood blocks between the tractor pieces so it stands. Glue the windows to the tractor, the hubcaps to the wheels, and the wheels to the tractor. Make sure the wheels are even so the tractor stands upright. Glue the tops of the tractor together.

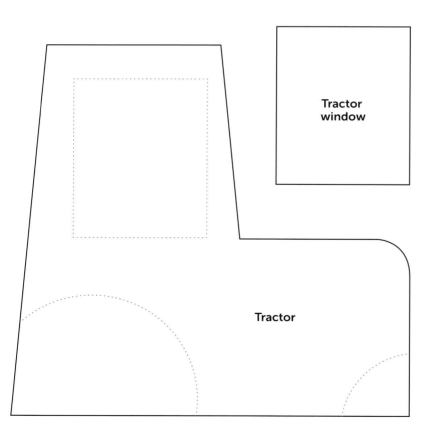

Tractor window

Tractor

Tractor front tire

Tractor front hubcap

Tractor back hubcap

Tractor back tire

SNORTING PIG

Here, little piggy! Is this the littlest pig or the one that went to the market? The decision is yours.

- Craft foam (9" x 12" sheets):
  - 1 pink (cut 1 each pig body, pig head, pig nose, and animal stand)
  - 1 chartreuse green, for grass
- 1 (1½") pink chenille stem
- Lamp black acrylic paint
- Stylus or toothpick

Note: See page 127 for the templates.

1. Trace and cut out the template pieces from the appropriate foam colors.

2. Paint the eyebrows, ear marks, and nostrils lamp black. Use a stylus or a toothpick and lamp black acrylic paint to dot on the eyes.

3. Curl the chenille stem around a pencil and glue it to the upper rear section of the body. Glue the two body sections together. Glue the nose to the head and the head to the body.

4. Cut "V"s into the chartreuse green craft foam piece for grass. Glue the grass to each side of the slit. Insert the stand into the slit.

CLUCKING CHICKEN

Here, chick, chick, chick! This chicken doesn't give you eggs, but it will put a smile to your face! The fun, feathery tail will be a great addition to your foamy farm.

- Craft foam (9" x 12" sheets):
  - 1 white (cut 1 each chicken head, chicken body, chicken back, and animal stand)
  - 1 yellow (cut 1 chicken beak)
  - 1 red (cut 1 chicken comb)
  - 1 chartreuse green, for grass
- 1 white boa feather

Note: See page 127 for the templates.

1. Glue the comb to the back of the head, the bill to the front of the head, the head to the body, the back to the body, and the feather to the back.

2. Use a fine-tip marker to dot in two eyes and add eyebrows and nostrils.

3. Insert the stand into the slit. Cut "V"s into the green strip for grass and glue it to the base of the chicken on each side of the slit.

KITTY CAT

Here, kitty, kitty! This cat is so friendly to have around your farm and so good at chasing away mice.

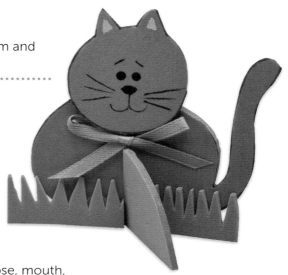

- Craft foam (9" x 12" sheets):
  - 1 gray (cut 1 each cat head, cat body, and animal stand)
  - 1 chartreuse green, for grass
- ⅛"-wide pink satin ribbon, 4" long
- Acrylic paint: bubblegum pink and lamp black
- Fine-tip marker
- Stylus or toothpick

1. Trace and cut out the template pieces from the appropriate foam colors.

2. Use a fine-tip marker to draw the ears, eyebrows, eyes, nose, mouth, and whiskers on the head.

3. Paint the inside of the ears bubblegum pink and the eyebrows, mouth, and whiskers lamp black. Use a stylus or toothpick and lamp black to dot on eyes. Glue the head to the body.

4. Insert the stand into the slit. Clip "V"s from the chartreuse green craft foam strip for grass and glue to each side of the slit.

WOOLY SHEEP

Baaaaa! This wooly sheep is a little wild, but very friendly. You'll enjoy having him on your farm.

- Craft foam (9" x 12" sheets):
  - 1 white (cut 1 each sheep body and animal stand)
  - 1 black (cut 1 sheep head)
  - 1 chartreuse green, for grass
- ½" white flower button
- Titanium white acrylic paint
- Stylus or toothpick
- Fine-tip marker

1. Trace and cut out the template pieces from the appropriate foam colors.

2. Use a stylus or toothpick and titanium white to dot on the eyes. Paint the white eyebrows. Use a fine-tip marker to draw curls on the front and back of the body.

3. Glue a button to the head and the head to the body. Insert the stand into the slit.

4. Cut "V"s into the chartreuse green craft foam piece for grass and glue it to each side of the slit.

Farm Animal Templates

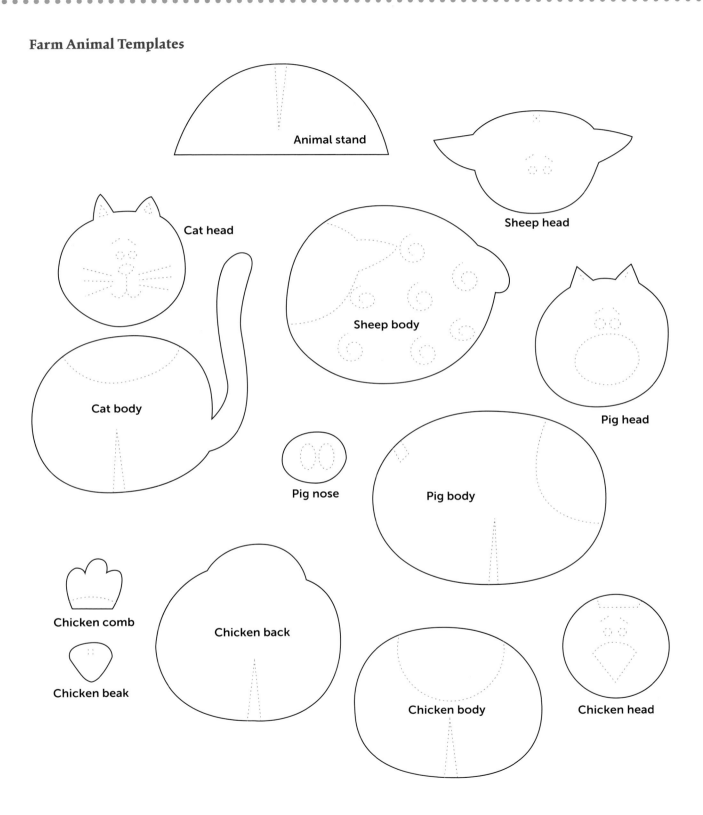

Animal stand

Sheep head

Cat head

Sheep body

Pig head

Cat body

Pig nose

Pig body

Chicken comb

Chicken beak

Chicken back

Chicken body

Chicken head

ANIMAL GIFT BOXES

Colorful and clever gift boxes will delight pet lovers of all ages that the box is basically a gift, too! You can place any small gift in the box, such as jewelry.

For the Brown Dog:

- 1 (2½" x 3") rounded rectangular papier-mâché box
- Craft foam:
  - Brown rectangles (cut 2 dog ears)
  - Large white circles (cut 2 animal cheeks)
  - 1 (¾") black ball, for nose
- 2 (10-mm) wiggle eyes
- Fine-tip black marker
- Acrylic paint: light brown and red

For the Gray Mouse:

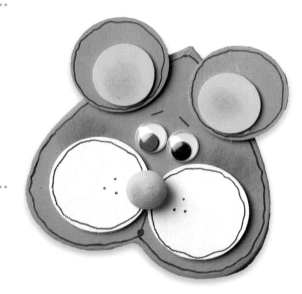

- 1 (2" x 3") heart papier-mâché box
- Craft foam:
  - Large gray circles (cut 2 mouse ears)
  - Small pink circles (cu 2 mouse inner ears)
  - Large white circles (cut 2 animal cheeks)
  - 1 (⅝" diameter) pink ball, for nose
- 2 (10-mm) wiggle eyes
- Fine-tip black marker
- Acrylic paint: gray and red

For the Orange Cat:

- 1 (2" x 3") oval papier-mâché box
- Craft foam:
  - Pink triangle (cut 1 cat nose)
  - Yellow triangle (cut 2 cat ears)
  - Large white circles (cut 2 animal cheeks)
- 2 (10-mm) wiggle eyes
- Fine-tip black marker
- Acrylic paint: yellow-orange and red

TIP: Dry-brush inner ears and nose with red paint.

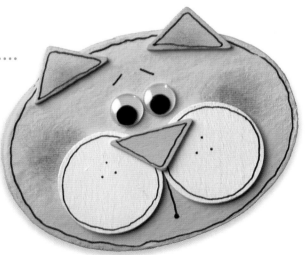

1. Paint the box. Let it dry.

2. Dry brush the cheeks on the box with red paint.

3. Outline the box lid and foam pieces with a black marker.

4. Glue the foam pieces and eyes to the box.

5. Draw the face lines with a black marker.

Animal Gift Boxes Templates

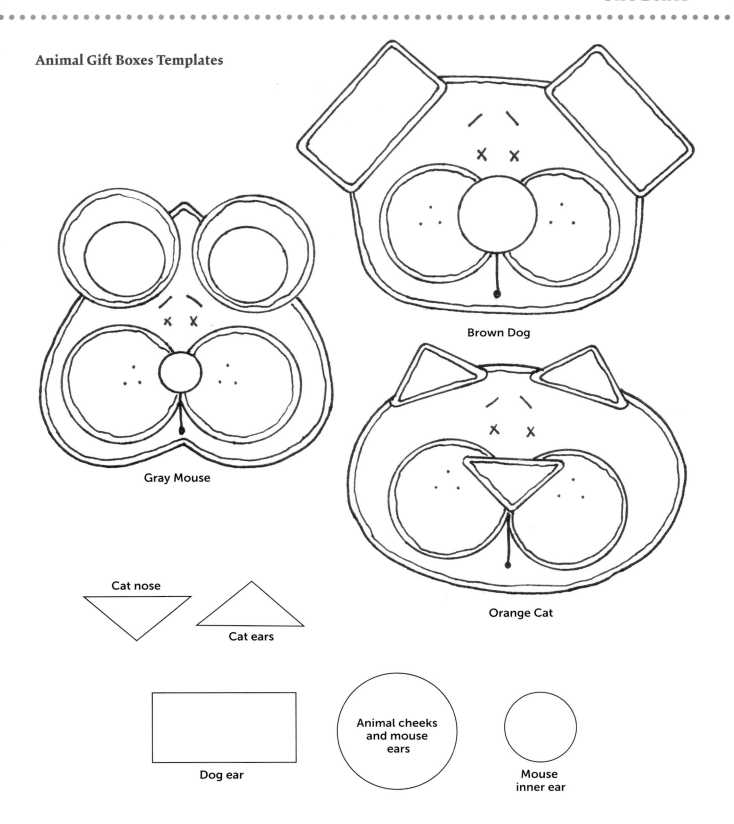

Brown Dog

Gray Mouse

Orange Cat

Cat nose

Cat ears

Dog ear

Animal cheeks and mouse ears

Mouse inner ear

WIGGLY JELLYFISH BOX

Add personality and an ocean theme to an ordinary gift box. Make it even more beautiful by adhering seashells around the bottom or handle. Use this attractive container to hold pencils or keepsakes. Set it on the television to hold remotes or place it beside your fish tank to neatly store fish food bottles.

- 1 (2" x 4⅛" x 6") wooden box with handle
- 1 (1¼" x 2¾") pink foam oval for jellyfish
- Fern chunky stamp
- Paintbrush
- 2 (7-mm) wiggle eyes
- ⅛"-wide ribbon, 12" long: 1 coral and 1 cream
- Fine-tip black marker
- Acrylic paint: white, blue, dark green, and light green
- Paper towel

1. Cut the ribbons into 3" sections.

2. Paint the box. Let it dry.

3. Use a crinkled paper towel to dab white paint over the oval (A). Let it dry.

4. Apply paint to the stamp with a paintbrush (B). Stamp on the box (C).

5. Outline the top of the box, the box handle, and the jellyfish with black marker.

6. Using the rounded end of a paintbrush handle, randomly dot all sides of the box with white paint to make air bubbles.

7. Glue eyes to jellyfish. Glue ribbons to the back of the jellyfish. Glue the jellyfish to the box.

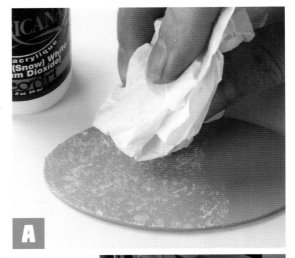

A

B

C

GLITTERY STAR PURSE

The only thing better than carrying a sparkly star purse like this one is making it yourself! Show off your crafty talents by carrying this beautiful and sparkly purse everywhere you go.

- Craft foam:
  - 1 (9" x 12" sheet) purple glitter (cut 2 purses)
  - 2 gold glitter stars (2¼" precut or cut star B's)
  - 4 gold glitter stars (1" precut or cut star A's)
- 1 yard of ¹⁄₁₆" lavender sparkly silky cord
- 1" piece of hook-and-loop tape

1. Referring to the pattern, use a paper punch to make holes approximately ³⁄₁₆" from the outside edge of the two purse A rectangle templates.

2. Adhere 2 small stars and 1 large star to each glitter foam side.

3. Use a silky cord and go in and out of the punched holes to lace the sections together. Glue the cord ends to the inside.

4. Cut a 1" x 11" strip from the purple glitter foam and glue to the purse sections for the handle; use clothespins to hold the pieces together until it's dry.

5. Glue a piece of hook-and-loop tape to the top edge on each inside section in the center.

Star A template

Star B template

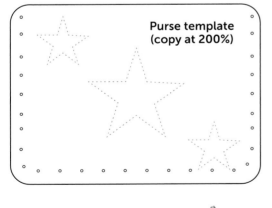

Purse template (copy at 200%)

MULTICOLORED PURSE

This first bag uses a lot of the techniques that you'll use for the bags that follow. You can make a lovely purse to carry around makeup, accessories, electronics, or other goodies. You'll want to take your new bag everywhere!

- Craft foam (3 mm thick):
  - 1 (6" x 12") lime, for bag body
  - 1 (1" x 12") lime, for strap
  - 1 (5" x 6") pink, for flap
  - 1 (½" x 12") pink, for strap accent strip
  - 1 (1" x 6") pink, for inside reinforcement strip
  - 1 (1" x 6") white, for flap accent strip
- Craft foam (5 mm thick):
  - 2 white (cut 1 purse bag side)
- Decorative brads
- Adhesive-backed foam shapes
- Hook-and-loop adhesive dots
- Large needle or awl

Note: See page 135 for the templates.

1. Collect all materials and cut out all foam pieces according to the cutting chart (A).

2. Apply adhesive to the side and bottom edges of one bag side piece at a time (B).

3. Working in 2" sections, press the long edge of the bag body into the adhesive, wrapping it around three edges of one bag side piece at a time. Hold until the adhesive sets (C). The bag body will extend about 1½" past the bag sides at the back.

4. Apply adhesive to the flap accent strip, and attach it to the bottom front edge of the flap (D).

5. Apply adhesive to the underside of the flap on the opposite side from the accent strip, and attach it to the bag body, overlapping the two edges 1½" for support (E). You can also use brads to attach the flap if desired.

6. Apply adhesive to the inside reinforcement strip, and attach it to the inside of the bag body, even with the top edge of the back of the bag as shown (F). (If you choose to use brads to attach the flap, this will cover up their ends. Read more about using brads on page 22)

7. Apply adhesive to the back of the strap accent strip, and attach it to the center of the strap (G).

8. Using an awl or large needle, poke a hole through each bag side at the position marked on the bag side pattern (H). You can mark it with pen first, because the hole and the pen mark will be covered up. Children should get help from an adult for this step.

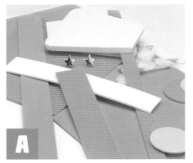
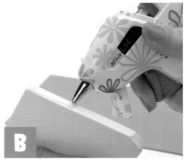

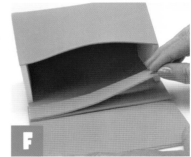

9. Insert brads through the ends of completed strap and then through the holes in the bag sides, and open the ends of the brads (I). The strap foam should be thin enough that you can push the brad through without punching a hole.

10. Cover the brad ends on both sides with a 1"-diameter adhesive-backed circle (J).

11. Apply one half of a hook-and-loop adhesive dot to the underside of the flap and the other half to the front of the bag body for the closure (K).

12. Embellish the flap as desired (L).

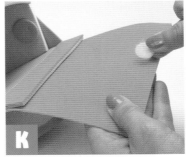

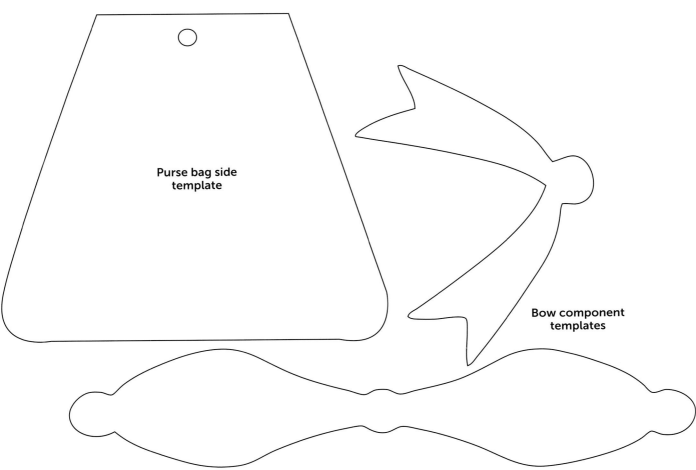

Purse bag side template

Bow component templates

HANDY TOOLBOX

If you like to help your parents fix things around the house, make this toolbox to keep all your tools in one place. You could even fit a small—but handy—flashlight in this bag! The construction of this toolbox is very similar to the Multicolored Purse on page 133.

- ● **Craft foam (3 mm thick):**
  - ■ **1 (6" x 12") dark brown, for bag body**
  - ■ **1 (1" x 12") dark brown, for strap**
  - ■ **1 dark brown (cut 1 hammer template)**
  - ■ **1 (5" x 6") light brown, for flap**
  - ■ **1 (1" x 6") light brown, for inside reinforcement strip**
  - ■ **1 (1" x 6") teal, for flap accent strip**
  - ■ **1 teal (cut 1 hammer template)**
- ● **Craft foam (5 mm thick):**
  - ■ **2 white (cut 1 toolbox bag side)**
- ● **Decorative brads**
- ● **Adhesive-backed tool-themed foam shapes**
- ● **Hook-and-loop adhesive dots**
- ● **Large needle or awl**

Note: See page 137 for the templates.

1. Collect all materials and cut out all foam pieces according to the cutting chart.

2. Apply hot glue to the side and bottom edges of one white bag side piece at a time.

3. Working in 2" sections, press the long edge of the dark brown bag body into the adhesive, wrapping it around three edges of one white bag side piece at a time. Hold until the glue sets. The bag body will extend about 1½" past the bag sides at the back.

4. Apply glue to the teal flap accent strip, and attach it to the bottom front edge of the light brown flap.

5. Apply glue to the underside of the light brown flap on the opposite side from the accent strip, and attach it to the bag body, overlapping the two edges 1½" for support. You can also use brads to attach the flap if desired.

6. Apply adhesive to the light brown inside reinforcement strip, and attach it to the inside of the dark brown bag body, even with the top edge of the back of the bag as shown. (If you choose to use brads to attach the flap, this will cover up their ends. Read more about using brads on page 22).

7. Using an awl or large needle, poke a hole through each white bag side at the position marked on the bag side pattern. It's advised that you mark it with pen first since the hole and the pen mark will be covered up. Children should get help from an adult for this step.

8. Insert brads through the ends of dark brown strap and then through the holes in the bag sides, and open the ends of the brads. The strap foam should be thin enough that you can push the brad through without punching a hole.

9. Cover the brad ends on both sides with a 1"-diameter adhesive-backed circle.

10. Apply one half of a hook-and-loop adhesive dot to the underside of the light brown flap and the other half to the front of the bag body for the closure.

11. Place the teal hammer handle and the dark brown hammerhead on the middle of the bag at an angle. Next, place the brown hammer handle and the teal hammerhead on top of the first hammer at an opposite angle. Stick some adhesive tool-themed foam shapes on the accent flap.

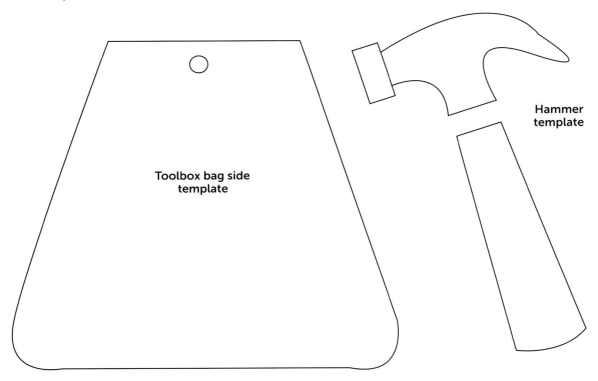

Toolbox bag side template

Hammer template

CONTRAST PENCIL CASE/CLUTCH

Whether you make a vibrantly patterned clutch that is perfect for dress-up, or a cool geometric personalized pencil case, everyone will be amazed at your unique style.

- Craft foam (3 mm thick):
  - 1 (12" x 7") print, for clutch body
  - 2 (¾" x 12") print, for side accent strip
  - 1 (¼" x 4") print, for inside pocket accent strip
  - 1 (¾" x 12") print, for strap
  - 1 (3" x 4") solid color, for inside pocket
  - 1 (¼" x 11") solid color, for strap accent strip
- Craft foam (5 mm thick):
  - 2 (1" x 3½") black, for clutch
- Swivel clip
- D-ring
- Hook-and-loop adhesive dots

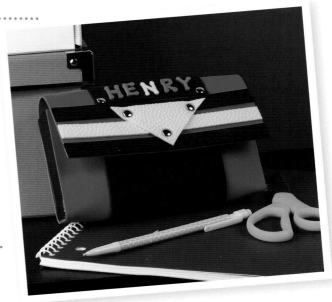

1. Collect all materials and cut out all foam pieces according to the cutting chart (A).

2. Apply adhesive to the side and bottom edges of one clutch side piece at a time. Working in 2" sections, press the long edges of the clutch body into the adhesive, wrapping it around the three edges of one clutch side piece at a time (B). The bag body will extend past the bag sides at the back to form the flap. Hold until the adhesive sets.

3. Apply adhesive to the inside pocket accent strip, and attach it to the front top edge of the inside pocket (C).

4. Apply adhesive to the back of the inside pocket along the sides and bottom (D).

5. Attach the pocket to the inside of the clutch as shown, centering it ½" down from the top of the side pieces of the clutch (E).

6. Slide the D-ring onto one side accent strip, fold the strip over 1½", and glue the folded piece down (F).

7. Apply adhesive to one clutch side and press the side accent strip into the adhesive, letting the end with the D-ring extend 1" above the top edge of the clutch (G). Continue adding adhesive and pressing the side accent strip into the clutch side, working in 2" sections at a time.

8. Continue attaching the side accent strip along the bottom of the clutch, adding more adhesive as you go until you reach the end of the strip (H).

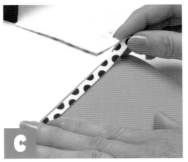

9. Butt the end of the second side accent strip up to the end of the first strip and continue adding adhesive and pressing it in place around the bottom of the clutch and up the opposite side (I).

10. Trim away any excess from the second side accent strip, even with the top edge of the clutch side (J).

11. Slide the swivel clip onto the strap, fold the strap over 1", and glue the folded piece down (K).

12. Apply adhesive directly below the folded and glued end of the strap, bring the opposite end up into a loop, and press it down onto the adhesive, aligning it with the edge of the folded portion (L).

13. Apply adhesive to the strap accent strip and attach it to the center of the strap, wrapping it around the entire strap until the ends meet (M).

14. Clip the strap onto the body of the clutch (N).

15. Apply hook-and-loop adhesive dots for the closure, and embellish with foam shapes and adhesive accents as desired (O).

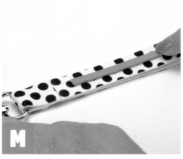

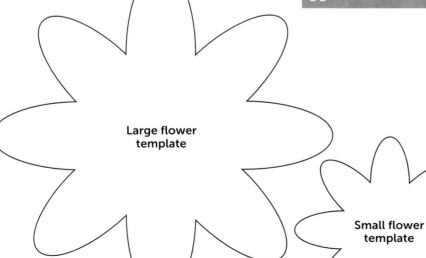

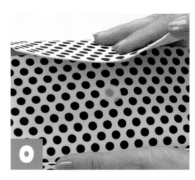

Large flower template

Small flower template

FLORAL BAG CHARM

Decorate a backpack or lunch bag, or use it as a zipper pull.
All you need is some foam and some ribbon.

- **Adhesive-backed foam shapes**
- **⅛"-wide black satin ribbon, 10" long**
- **1 black pom-pom**

1. Remove the paper backing from one foam shape and, with the ribbon folded in half, press the ribbon into the adhesive so that the ribbon loop extends beyond the top of the shape (A). You can leave a decorative tail by letting the two loose ribbon ends stick out, or hide them inside the shape.

2. Remove the paper backing from a second adhesive foam shape and press it onto the back of the first shape, sandwiching the ribbon (B).

3. Apply adhesive to the back of a pom-pom and press it in the center of the front of the bag charm (C). You can add other embellishments, too (like the extra white flower in the photo). To attach your charm, simply loop the ribbon through and tie it to a zipper or bag handle.

FUNKY CHAIN MESSENGER BAG

The ultimate handy accessory for any student or adventurer is a large messenger bag with a long strap that can carry whatever you need. Mix prints for funky combinations, decorate with patriotic stars—the possibilities are endless.

- ● **Craft foam (3 mm thick):**
  - ■ 1 print (cut 1 messenger bag front flap)
  - ■ 1 (1" x 7½") print, for front accent strip
  - ■ 1 (3" x 2½") print, for side pocket
  - ■ 1 (3" x 4½") print, for inside pocket
  - ■ 1 (7½" x 11½") yellow, for bag body
  - ■ 2 (½" x 8") yellow, for strap loops
  - ■ 1 (1" x 8") yellow, for front fastener tab
  - ■ 1 (1" x 4") yellow, for front fastener loop
  - ■ 1 (¼" x 4½") yellow, for inside pocket accent strip
- ● **Craft foam (5 mm thick):**
  - ■ 2 white pieces (cut 2 messenger bag sides)
- ● **Adhesive-backed metallic accents**
- ● **Plastic chain link**
- ● **Fine-tip marker**

Note: See page 147 for the templates.

1. Collect all materials and cut out all foam pieces according to the cutting chart (A).

2. Apply adhesive to the side and bottom edges of one side piece. Working in 2" sections, press one long edge of the bag body into the adhesive, wrapping it around the three edges of the side piece (B). Hold until the adhesive sets.

3. Repeat for the opposite side of the bag. When finished, the bag body will extend past the top of the bag sides at the back (you can see this in the background of the photo) (C).

4. Apply adhesive to the inside pocket accent strip. Attach the strip to the front of the inside pocket ¼" down from the top edge (D).

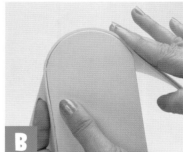

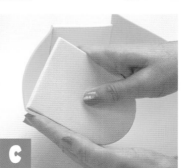

5. Apply adhesive to the back of the inside pocket along the sides and bottom. Attach the pocket to the inside of the bag body, centering it 1" down from the top edge (E).

6. Apply adhesive to the underside of the front flap along the straight edge, and attach the flap to the top edge of the bag body that extends past the sides of the bag, overlapping by 1" for support (F).

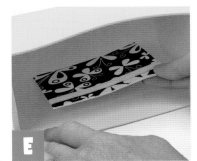
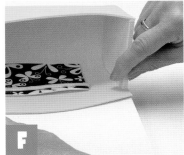

7. Apply adhesive to the front accent strip. Attach the strip to the front of the bag body, even with the top edge (G).

8. Apply adhesive to the back of the front fastener tab and fold the ends in toward the center so the edges meet. Press it flat (H). This makes the tab double-layered for extra strength.

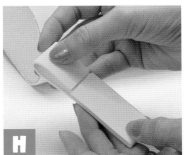

9. Add decorative stitching lines to the tab with a fine-tip marker (I).

10. Attach adhesive-backed metallic accents to the tab (J).

11. Apply adhesive to about half of the back of the tab and attach it to the center front of the front flap, 2" up from the bottom edge (K).

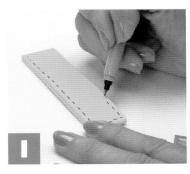

12. Apply adhesive to each end of the front fastener loop and attach it to the front of the bag, centering it 1½" below the front accent strip (L). It is helpful to hold the flap with the tab down so that you can glue the fastener loop over the tab and align it correctly.

13. Check to make sure you can slide the tab in and out of the loop without too much trouble (M).

14. Apply adhesive to one of the strap loops and attach it the other to make a double-layered single piece (N). Then cut the piece in half so that you have two 4"-long pieces.

15. Fold one 4" piece into a loop as shown (O). If you are using a chain or other material that can't be opened and closed, slide the strap onto the loop prior to gluing it to the bag. Apply adhesive to the bottom of each side of the loop and attach it to one side of the bag, about 2" down from the top edge.

16. Apply adhesive to the back of the side pocket along the sides and bottom and glue it to the bag side, over the strap loops and ½" down from the top edge (P).

17. Attach the chain to the strap loop (Q).

18. Use the other 4" piece from step 14 to make the loop on the other side of the bag. Here you can see the other side of the bag, without a pocket (R).

M

N

O

P

Q

R

GINGHAM MESSENGER BAG

This version of the messenger bag is put together in much the same way as the first, but has some important decorative and functional differences. Make both, or mix and match features from each bag to create a whole new style!

- **Craft foam (3 mm thick):**
  - 1 (7½" x 11½") black, for bag body
  - 1 (7½" x 5") yellow, for front flap
  - 1 (1½" x 18") yellow, for straps
  - 1 (¼" x 18") yellow, for strap accent strips
  - 1 (1½" x 2") yellow, for strap reinforcement
  - 2 (¼" x 11½") yellow, for bag accent strips
  - 1 (2½" x 3") yellow, for inside pocket
  - 1 (1½" x 16") white, for inside bag reinforcement strap
- **Craft foam (5 mm thick):**
  - 2 white (cut 2 messenger bag sides)
- **Adhesive-backed metallic accents**
- **Adhesive-backed foam shapes**
- **Hook-and-loop adhesive dots**

Note: See page 147 for the templates.

1. Collect all materials and cut out all foam pieces according to the cutting chart (A).

2. Apply adhesive to the bag accent strips and attach them to the long edges of the bag body, ⅛" in along each side (B).

3. Apply adhesive to the back of the inside pocket along the sides and bottom, and attach it to one of the bag sides, centering the pocket ½" down from the top edge (C).

4. Apply adhesive to the side and bottom edges of one bag side piece. Working in 2" sections, press one long edge of the bag body into the adhesive, wrapping it around the three edges of the side piece (D). Hold until the adhesive sets.

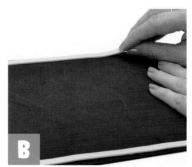

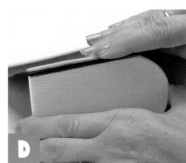

5. Repeat for the opposite side of the bag. When finished, the bag body will extend ½" past the top of the bag sides at the back (E). Be sure to attach the bag side that has the pocket so that the pocket is inside of the bag.

6. Apply adhesive to the underside of the front flap along one of the long edges and attach it to the top edge of the bag body that extends past the sides of the bag, overlapping by ½" for support (F).

7. Apply adhesive to the bag reinforcement strip and attach it to the inside of the bag, centering the strip as shown (G). If gluing, do only half of the strip at a time, starting by applying glue to the part of the strip on the inside of the bag, pressing it down, and then applying glue on the part of the strip that attaches to the flap.

8. Butt the two straps together end to end. Then, apply adhesive to the strap reinforcement and attach it over the place where the two strap pieces touch (H). This connects them to create one long strap.

9. Cut two of the strap accent strips in half, so that you end up with four short strips and two long strips (uncut). Apply adhesive to one short strip, align one end with one end of the strap, and attach it along the long edge (I). Apply adhesive to a long strip, butt it against the short strip you just attached, and attach it. Then, attach another short strip butted against the other end of the long strip. This will complete an accent strip that runs the length of the entire strap. Repeat with the remaining strips for the other side of the strap. This cutting method is used to avoid a seam on top of a seam at the center of the strap.

10. Apply adhesive to the underside of the ends of the strap and attach them to the bag sides (J).

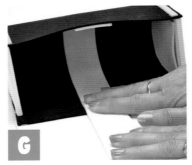

11. Apply three hook-and-loop adhesive dots to the bag flap and the body of the bag for the closure (K).

12. Embellish with foam shapes and metallic accents (L).

Messenger Bag Templates

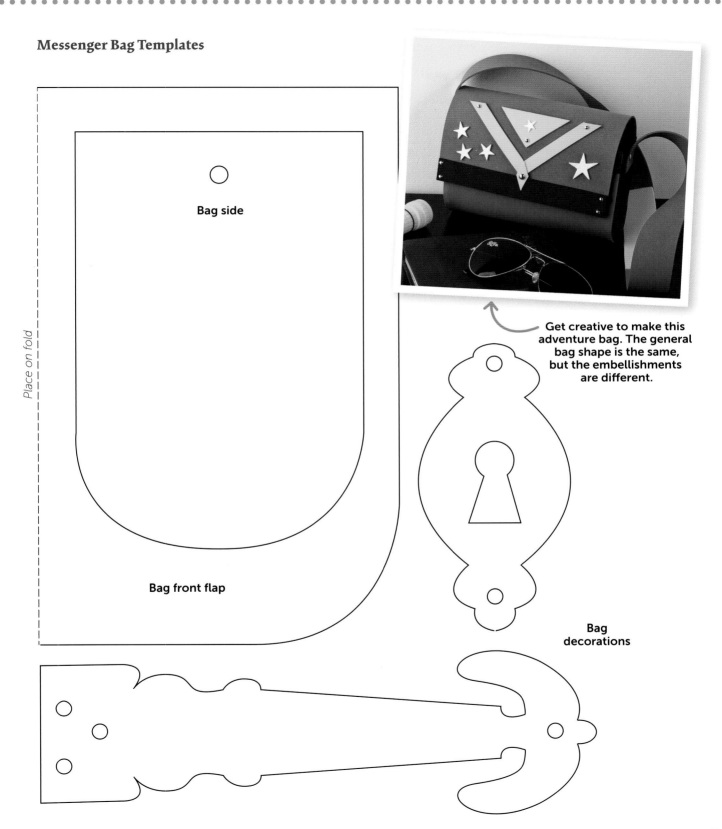

Place on fold

Bag side

Bag front flap

Get creative to make this adventure bag. The general bag shape is the same, but the embellishments are different.

Bag decorations

FRINGED TASSEL

A colorful tassel will jazz up anything that needs a little pizzazz. It may look tricky to make, but it's really quite simple.

- **Craft foam (3 mm thick):**
  - 1 (1½" x 5") yellow, for tassel
  - 1 (¼" x 2½") print, for accent strip
- **¼"-wide black satin ribbon, 6" long**
- **Plastic beads**

1. Collect all materials and cut out all foam pieces according to the cutting chart (A).

2. Cut into the long edge of tassel piece with repeated cuts ¼" apart, cutting along the entire 5" length. Leave a ¼" of the strip intact along the top edge (B).

3. Apply adhesive all along the uncut top edge of the tassel, fold the ribbon in half, and press it into the adhesive so the loop of the ribbon extends 1" down from the glue (C).

4. Start rolling the tassel, beginning at the end with the ribbon (D). The two loose ribbon ends stick out of the top of the tassel so that it can be tied on to anything.

5. Apply adhesive to the accent strip and wrap it around the top of the tassel, trimming away any excess (E).

6. Slide several beads onto the two ribbon ends, and add some dots of glue to the ribbon at the base of the tassel. Slide the beads down over top of the glue (F). This will keep the beads together and keep them down against the tassel.

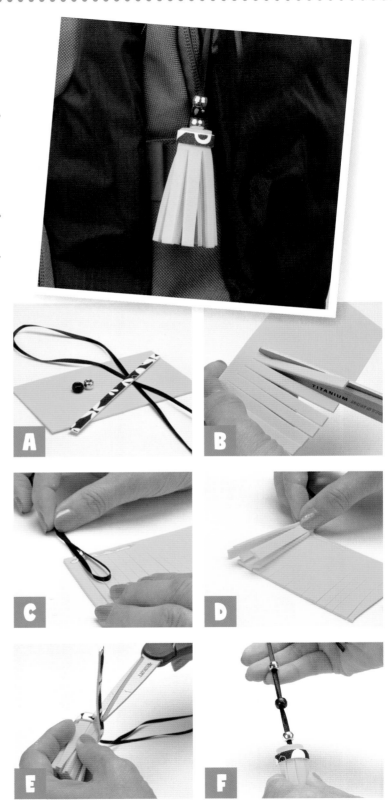

EMBELLISHED KEY FOB

This key fob can be used for keys or just attached to a backpack or other accessory as decoration. Use your initial to show the world it is your creation.

- Craft foam (3 mm thick):
  - 1 blue (cut 1 key fob)
  - 1 yellow (with adhesive back) (cut 1 key fob)
- Adhesive-backed foam letter
- ⅜"-wide grosgrain ribbon, 4" long
- Plastic swivel clip
- Key ring
- Fine-tip marker

Key fob template

TIP: Apply double-sided adhesive to the circle before cutting it out, if necessary.

1. Collect all materials and cut out all foam pieces according to the cutting chart (A).

2. Remove the paper backing from the foam letter and press it in place on top of the yellow adhesive-backed circle (B).

3. Attach the swivel clip to the key ring. Slide the key ring onto the ribbon and fold the ribbon in half to form a loop (C). Remove the paper backing from the yellow circle and press the ribbon ends into the adhesive, allowing the top loop to extend a bit beyond the edge of the circle.

4. Cover the back of the yellow circle with the blue circle, pressing them together to sandwich the ribbon (D).

5. Use a fine-tip marker to add stitching lines (E).

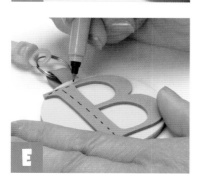

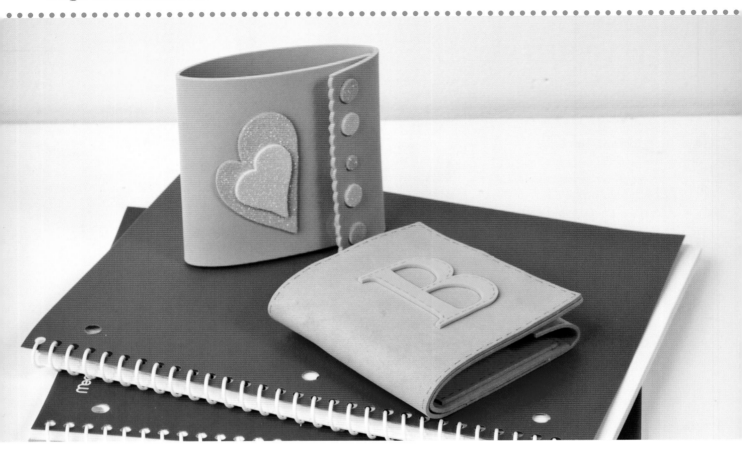

FOAMY WALLET

Just three pieces of foam and some decorations come together to make a perfectly functional wallet. Don't spend your money all in one place!

- **Craft foam (3 mm thick):**
  - 1 (4" x 10") blue, for wallet body
  - 1 (2½" x 8") blue, for large inside pocket
  - 1 (2" x 3") blue, for small inside pocket
- **Adhesive-backed foam letter**
- **Hook-and-loop adhesive dots**
- **Fine-tip marker**

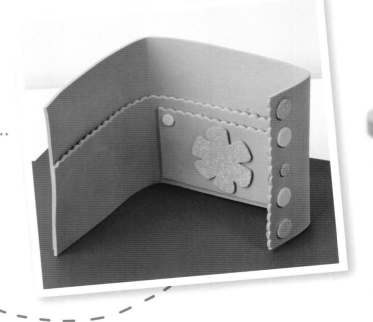

1. Collect all materials and cut out all foam pieces according to the cutting chart (A).

2. Apply adhesive to the back of the large inside pocket along the sides and bottom, as well as in a line in the center (B). Attach the pocket to the wallet body so it's even with the bottom left corner. In this photo you can see some double-sided adhesive tape on the foam piece, which is another option for adhesion.

3. Apply adhesive to the back of the small inside pocket along the sides and bottom. Attach it on top of the large pocket as shown (C).

4. Add hook-and-loop adhesive dots to the wallet for the closure (D).

5. You can decide how you want the wallet to fold depending on the placement of the dots (E). Here, the wallet folds over onto the outside front. You also have the option to fold the wallet on the inside so that you don't see a fold on the front of the wallet.

6. Embellish the outside of the wallet with an adhesive-backed foam letter, and add stitching lines to the letter and wallet using a fine-tip marker (F).

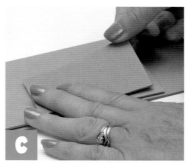

GEOMETRIC CARRYALL

This funky, modern design is perfect for carrying all the craft items you need to get creative, from small drawings and pens and pencils to scissors and other helpful tools. With a handy inner pocket and a secure strap, tote your supplies in style.

- Craft foam (3 mm thick):
  - 1 (8" x 15") purple, for bag body
  - 2 (½" x 15") purple, for handles
  - 1 (½" x 18") purple, for buckle strap
  - 1 (1½" x 3½") purple, for center pocket tab
  - 2 (6" x 5") assorted textured, for side pockets
  - 2 (6" x 8") assorted textured, for center pocket
  - 1 (1" x 8") assorted textured, for center spine
  - 1 (¾" x 8") assorted textured, for center spine reinforcement strip
- Plastic buckle closure
- 8 (½"-diameter) plastic rings
- Hook-and-loop adhesive dots
- 1 (¼"-diameter) hole punch

1. Collect all materials and cut out all foam pieces according to the cutting chart (A).

2. Mark the centerline of the bag body (at 7½") (B).

3. Apply adhesive to the center spine reinforcement strip and attach it in the center of the bag body, over the line you drew in step 1 (C).

4. Apply adhesive to the two long sides of one of the center pocket pieces and attach the second pocket piece on top (D).

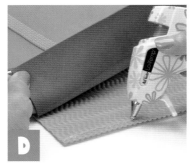

5. There will be an opening through the middle (E).

6. Center the pocket over the center spine. Apply adhesive to the center spine and press it over the pocket and center spine reinforcement strip (F).

7. Apply adhesive to one end of the center pocket tab and attach it to the center back of the left side of the pocket (G).

8. Apply hook-and-loop adhesive dots to the end of the tab and the back of the right side of the pocket (H).

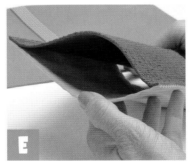

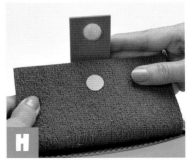

9. The pocket will close as shown (I).

10. Apply adhesive to the back of the two side pockets along the sides and bottom, and glue them to the inside of the bag body, one on each side of the center pocket. See the photo for placement (J).

11. Mark the placement for the handles at four spots by measuring 1" in from the bag's short sides and 1½" in from each of the bag's long sides. Use a hole punch to create four holes at the marked spots, two on each side of the bag (K).

12. Slide a plastic ring onto a handle piece, insert the handle into one of the holes made in step 10, slide a second ring onto the other side, and push the rings down next to the hole (L).

13. Then, fold the end of the handle over 1½" and glue it onto itself (M). Do this on the other end of the handle with the hole on the same side of the bag. Repeat with the remaining handle and two holes on the other side of the bag.

14. The rings reinforce the handle holes (N).

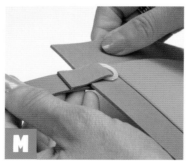

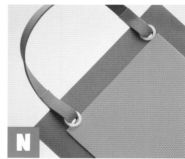

15. Center the buckle strap on the back of the bag so that equal lengths extend past the sides of the bag, and place it about 3" down from the top edge of the bag (O). Apply adhesive to attach it.

16. Slide one half of the buckle closure on one end of the buckle strap, fold the strap over about 1", and glue it down (P).

17. Take the other half of the buckle and clip the two buckle pieces together, then loop the other end of the strap through the other half of the buckle. Adjust the length of the strap to fit comfortably around the bag while the buckle is closed, fold over the end of the strap, and glue it down (Q).

18. Embellish with random cuts from textured craft foam, foam shapes, or other accents as desired (R).

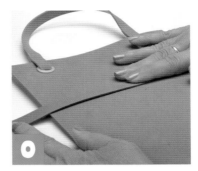
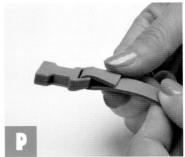
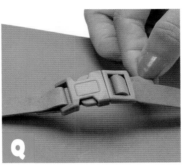
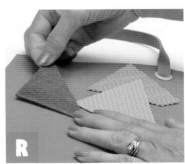

TEXTURED BELT POCKET

Sometimes you need easy access to those important things and just don't have pockets in your jeans! So here is a sturdy and stylish contraption that you slide onto your belt. Nifty!

- ● Craft foam (3 mm thick):
  - ■ 1 (3½" x 6") textured blue, for pocket front
  - ■ 2 (1" x 8½") textured blue, for pocket straps
  - ■ 1 (½" x 5½") textured blue, for inside reinforcement strip
  - ■ 1 (6" x 10") yellow, for pocket body
  - ■ 2 (1" x 2") yellow, for belt loop reinforcement strip
- ● Craft foam (5 mm thick):
  - ■ 2 (½" x 3½") white, for pocket side
- ● Decorative brads
- ● Hook-and-loop adhesive dots

1. Collect all materials and cut out all foam pieces according to the cutting chart (A).

2. Insert a brad into a pocket strap, 1" down from one end (B). Open the ends of the brad.

3. Apply adhesive to the end of the strap and fold it over, covering the end of brad (C). Repeat steps 1 and 2 for the second pocket strap.

4. Apply adhesive to the belt loop reinforcement strips and attach them to the back of the pocket straps, placing them 4" from the folded ends (D).

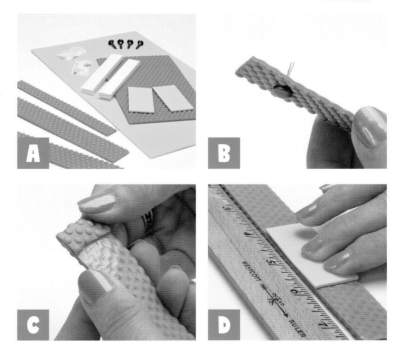

5. Apply adhesive to the back of the pocket straps, but not to the belt loop reinforcements (E). These are not glued down because they are where the belt will slide through.

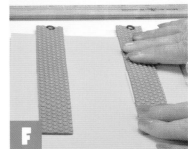

6. Press the straps in place on top of the pocket body, letting the top fold of each strap extend past the top edge of the pocket body. Place the straps 1" in from each long side of the pocket body (F).

7. Insert brads into the bottom ends of the pocket straps and through the pocket body (G).

8. Here you can see all four brads (H).

9. Apply adhesive to the side and bottom edges of one pocket side piece at a time and, working in 2" sections, press the long edges of the pocket body into the adhesive, wrapping it around the three sides of one side piece at a time. The pocket body will extend past the sides at the back to form the flap (you can see this in this photo) (I). Hold until the adhesive sets.

10. Apply adhesive to the inside reinforcement strip, and insert it inside the pocket to cover the brad ends along the bottom of the pocket (J).

11. Apply adhesive to the pocket front and press it to the front of the pocket body (K).

12. Apply hook-and-loop adhesive dots to the straps for the closure (L).

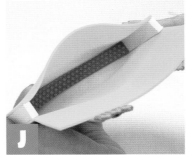

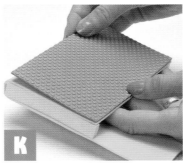

Index

A

accents, 16–18
accessories, 141, 148, 149
   See also magical accessories
adhesives, 10–14
angel finger puppet, 84, 86
animal gift boxes, 128–129
animal shapes
   foam, 68–69
   stitched, 70–71
apple tree, 121

B

bag charm, 141
bags
   belt pocket, 156–157
   carryall, 152–155
   clutch, 138–140
   messenger bag, 142–147
   pencil case, 138–140
   purses, 132–135
   toolbox, 136–137
   wallet, 150–151
barn template, 122–123
baseball template, 45
basketball template, 45
bat template, 45
bear finger puppet, 84, 86
belt pocket, 156–157
bird projects
   face masks, 91
   plant poke, 72
   valentine box, 106
blackboard project, 42–43
bracelets, 56, 99, 104
brads, 22
bug templates, 29
bumblebee pencil topper, 36
bunny projects
   Easter basket, 108
   finger puppet, 84, 86
   photo frame, 59
butterfly projects
   centerpiece, 46

crown, 48
foam shape, 69
headband bobbers, 102
mask, 49–50
napkin rings, 47
pencil favor, 47
pencil topper, 38
straw enhancement, 48
templates, 50, 51, 71

C

cards, 54, 105
carrot assembly, 59
carryall bag, 152–155
cars, 118–119
castle template, 31
cat projects
   boxes, 128–129
   face masks, 94–95
   finger puppet, 84
   foam cutout, 126
   photo frame, 57
caterpillar projects, 24, 25, 62
cereal box tracers, 15
chain messenger bag, 142–144
chicken cutout, 125, 127
classic car, 119
clutch bags, 138–140
coozie cup holder, 28, 112
cow, eye mask, 88–90
crown projects, 64, 100–101
cutting, 18–19

D

die cutters, 18
dog projects
   balancers, 86–87
   boxes, 128–129
   face masks, 93, 96
dolphin shapes, 68
door hanger, 66
double-sided adhesive sheets, 13
double-sided adhesive tape, 12
dragonfly projects, 74, 110–112

E

Easter bunny basket, 108
Easter egg holder, 109
embellishments, 16–18, 20, 23
eraser template, 42
eye masks, 88–90

F

face mask projects, 91–97
fairy door, 67
farm cutouts, 121–127
finger puppets, 82–86
firecracker hat, 113
fish projects, 41, 68, 70–71
flag template, 58
flower box, 35
flower party, 52–53
flower templates, 28, 32, 40, 50
flowers, foamy, 54–56
foam, craft, 10
football template, 45
frame template, 57
fringed tassel, 148
frog projects, 75, 78, 84, 86–87

G

gift boxes, 128–131
gingham messenger bag, 145–147
glasses, heart-shaped, 105
glue dots and lines, sticky, 13–14

H

headband bobbers, 102–103
heart projects, 50, 103, 105, 106–107
homemade cards, 54
hook-and-loop adhesive dots, 22

I

initial sign, 56

J

jack-o-lantern finger puppet, 84
jellyfish box, 130–131
journal, personalized, 26

K

key fob, 149
kid template, 42

L

ladybug projects
    photo frame, 59
    placemat, 110–111
    plant poke, 74
    visors, 24–25
leaf templates, 32, 40, 50
link chain, 67
lion finger puppet, 84

M

magical accessories, 98–104
magnetic photo frame, 57–59
message boards, 30, 42–44
messenger bag, 142–147
mini me blackboard project, 42–43
mouse assembly and template, 57,
    129
mouse boxes, 128–129
moving truck, 117
multicolored purse, 133

N

necklace, star, 98
notes message board, 30

P

pencil projects
    cases, 138–140
    embellishment, 47
    holders, 31–33
    toppers, 36, 38–41
pennant flag template, 45
photo keepers, 57–63
pig cutout, 125
plant pokes, 72–74
play mat, road, 114–115
princess face masks, 92, 96
princess room, 64–67
pumpkin wind socks, 76, 80

puppets, finger, 82–86
purple desk supplies, 30–31
purple pansy, 54
purses, 132–135

R

rabbit projects. *See* bunny projects
race car, 118
reindeer projects, 76, 79, 84, 86, 88,
    90
ring, star, 99
road play mat, 114–115
rollers, 19
royal crown, 100–101

S

sailboat, 120
Santa finger puppet, 84, 86
scrapbook page, 60
seahorse shapes, 68
sheep, 126
slithering snake box, 34
small children, projects for, 20
snowflake headband bobbers, 103
snowman finger puppet, 84, 86
soccer ball template, 45
sporty schedule holder, 44–45
star projects, 45, 51, 64, 98–101, 132
steam engine train & sign, 116
stitching projects, 28–29, 70–71

T

tassel, fringed, 148
tiara crown, 64
tiger masks, 88, 90
toolbox, 136–137
tractor, farm, 124
train & sign, 116
tropical wind sock, 77
turtle projects, 33, 39

V

vacation photo frame, 61
valentine birdie box, 106
valentine card, 105
visor projects
    all-tied-up, 26
    caterpillar, 24–25
    crafty visor, 28
    daffodil, 25
    flower frenzy, 27
    ladybug, 24–25, 74

W

wallet, 150–151
wand, star, 64, 100–101
wind socks, 75–81

Z

zebra wind socks, 75–76, 78

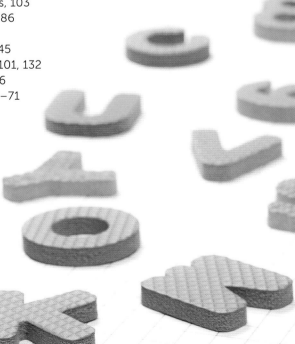

About the Contributors

Suzanne McNeill

Suzanne McNeill has received the "Lifetime Achievement Award" by the Craft & Hobby Association and had been noted as one of the arts and craft industry's top trendsetters. Dedicated to hands-on creativity, she is constantly testing, experimenting, and inventing something new and fun. Suzanne is the author of more than 230 craft and hobby books, and her creative vision has placed her books on the top of the trends for over 25 years.

Lorine Mason

Lorine Mason is a licensed product designer, an accomplished project designer, and the author of eleven how-to sewing and craft books, including *Making Jewelry with T-Shirt Yarn*. An eye for detail, innovative project design, trend awareness, and hard work are the cornerstones of her business, Lorine Mason Designs. Lorine loves all things crafty; while taking a break from sewing one day, she came upon the idea of crafting designer-style purses, wallets, and accessories for children. Utilizing craft foam, the perfect children's crafting medium, the projects in this book began to take form one at a time. Check out Lorine's blog at *www.lorinemason.com/blog*.

Margaret Riley

Margaret Riley is a successful designer, author, and teacher, and has done extensive work in editing, demonstrating, publishing, and manufacturing consulting. She formerly owned two hobby and craft stores and does features at trade shows and decorative art conventions throughout the U.S. She works in many fields that involve art, crafts, needlework, and food. When not in her studio, she enjoys riding a motorcycle and traveling in an RV with her husband. She adores her children, stepchildren, and grandchildren and shares her art talents with them. Creativity is her life!

Andrea Gibson

Andrea Gibson loves making things with her hands and sharing her creativity with others. The fun projects she created in this book were constructed with kids in mind to allow parents to enjoy some special bonding time with their kids. Andrea felt fortunate to have worked with her daughters Olivia, Ashton, and Michaella to develop her projects, and they wanted to share them with others so that they may have just as much fun.

The Longest
Strongest Thread

A book to share from
Scallywag Press

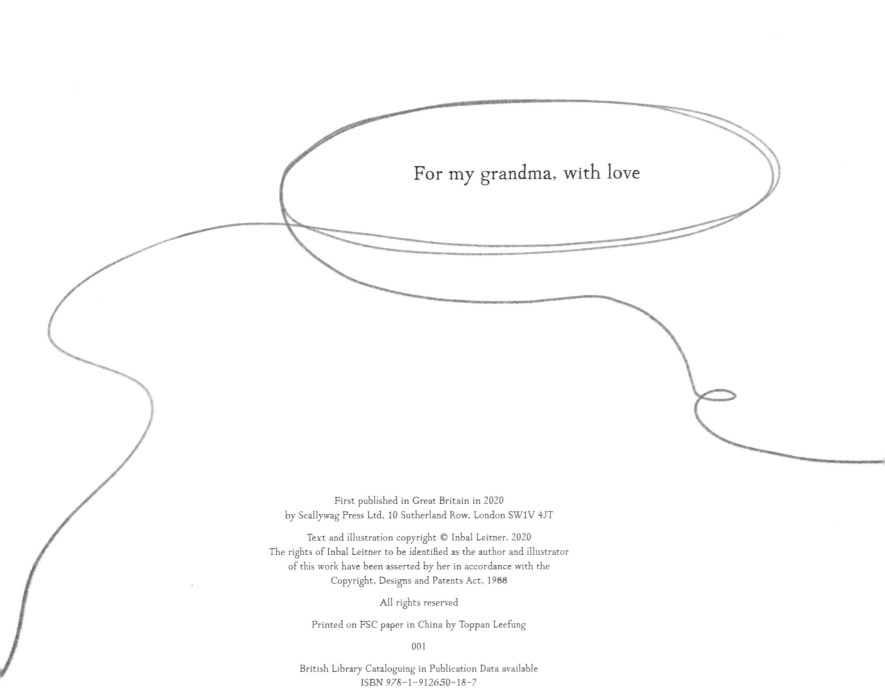

For my grandma, with love

First published in Great Britain in 2020
by Scallywag Press Ltd, 10 Sutherland Row, London SW1V 4JT

Text and illustration copyright © Inbal Leitner, 2020
The rights of Inbal Leitner to be identified as the author and illustrator
of this work have been asserted by her in accordance with the
Copyright, Designs and Patents Act, 1988

Printed on FSC paper in China by Toppan Leefung

001

British Library Cataloguing in Publication Data available
ISBN 978-1-912650-18-7

The Longest Strongest Thread

INBAL LEITNER

Scallywag Press Ltd
LONDON

This suitcase is SO HEAVY.

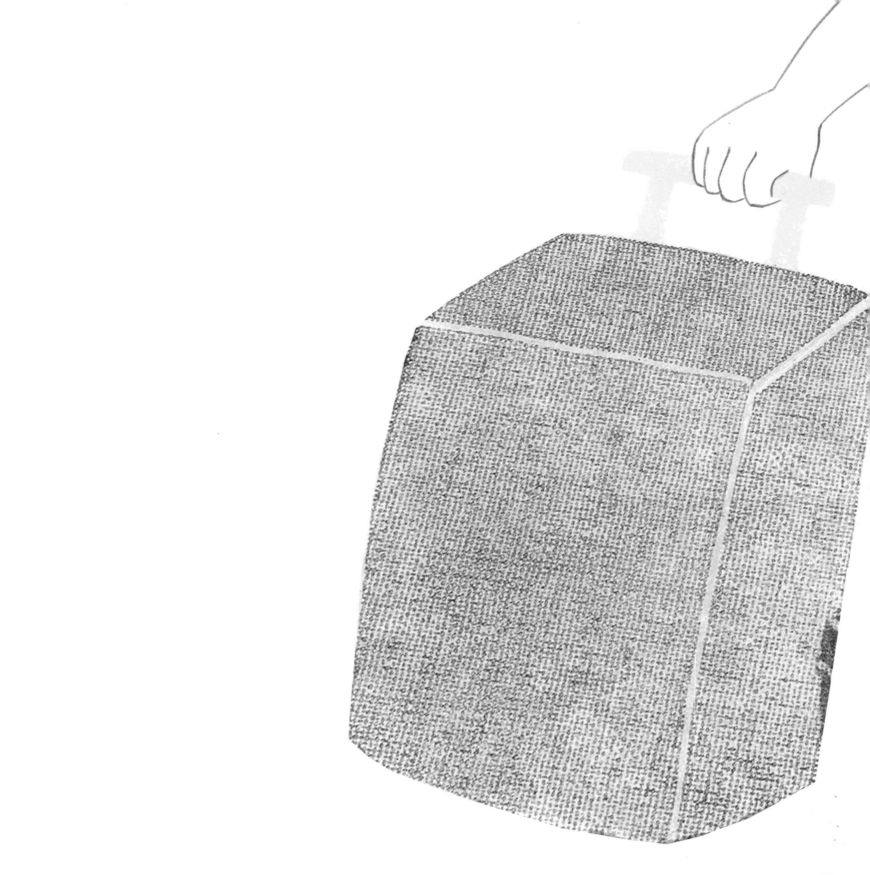

I think it has everything I'll need in my new home,
where the lakes freeze in winter.
We are flying there soon.

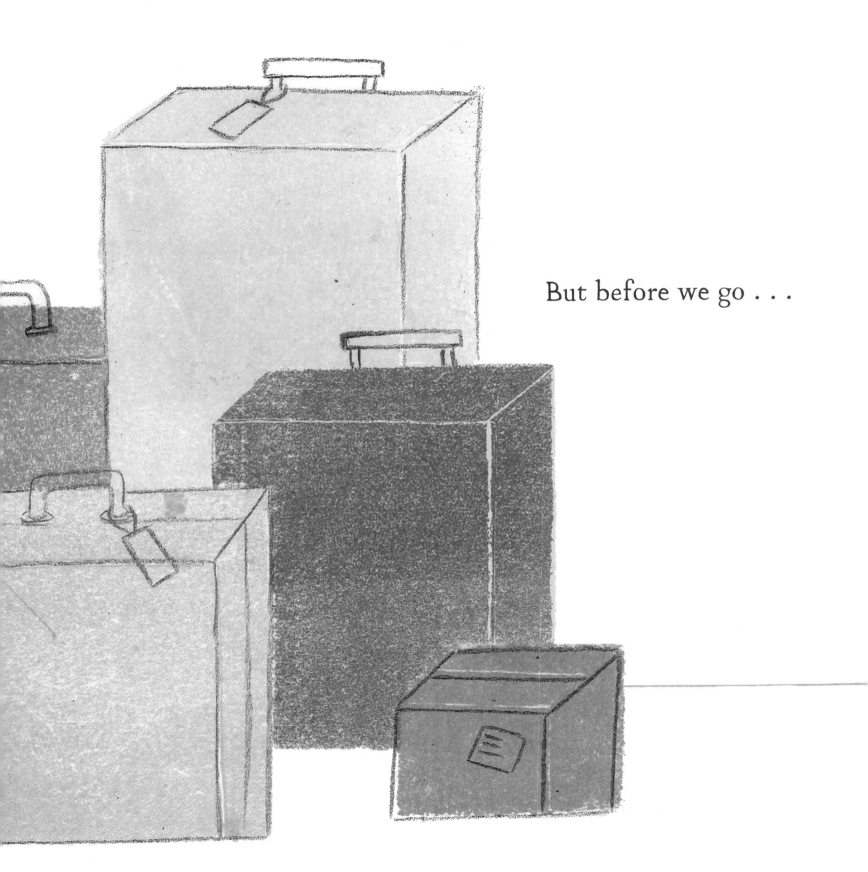

But before we go . . .

. . . I am visiting my Grandma to say goodbye.
I wish she could come too.

She is staying here where it is warm
and she has her sewing studio.

I LOVE Grandma's studio.

I help her choose
soft, warm fabric

and the strongest
blue thread.

My new home is very far away
from Grandma's studio.

I must draw her a map so she can find me . . .

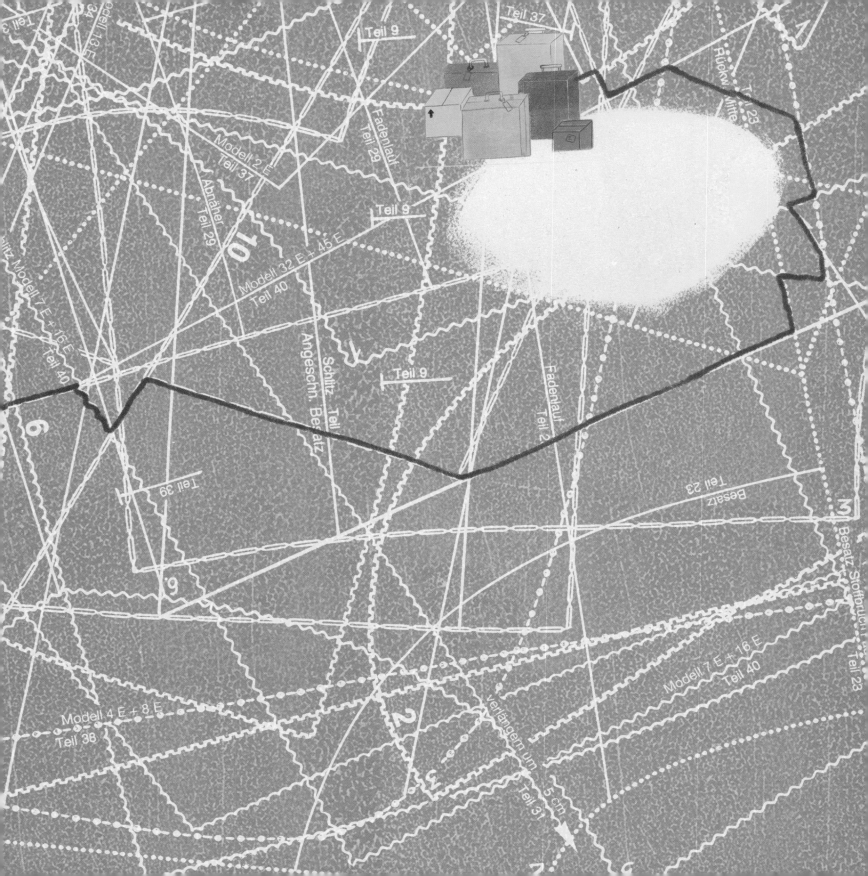

But even if she
knows where I am,

Grandma can't walk
all the way to my
new home.

So I am making her an aeroplane she can fly with.

If only there was an enormous pin magnet
I could use to pull her to me whenever I want.

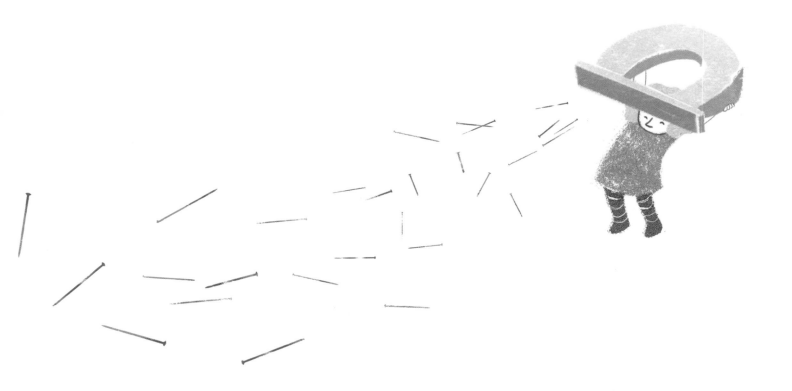

Grandma says I mustn't worry
that my new home is so very far away.

She says we two have the longest, strongest thread
in the whole world.

I love Grandma,

and Grandma
loves me.

We don't want to say goodbye.

But she promises me that when winter comes
and the lakes freeze . . .

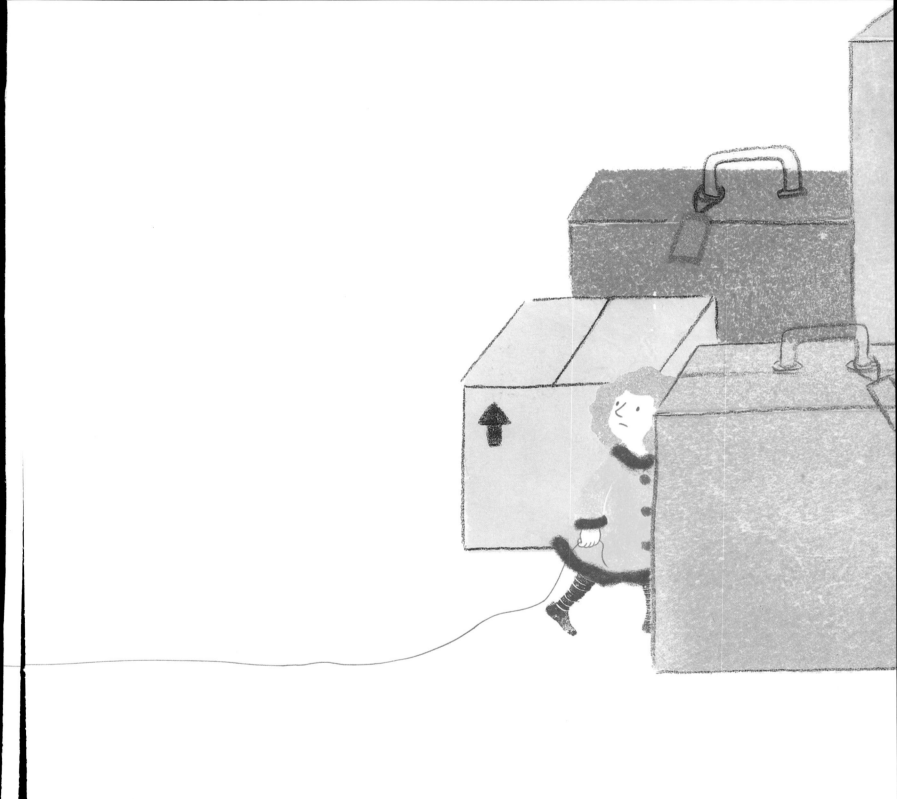

. . . she will surely use the map I gave her
and fly all the way to find me.